THE
NEXT MILE™

SHORT-TERM MISSIONS FOR THE LONG HAUL℠

GOER GUIDE

All-Age Edition

The Next Mile^{SM}

Short-Term Missons for the Long Haul^{SM}

GOER GUIDE

All-Age Edition

Authentic

Authentic

We welcome your comments and questions.
129 Mobilization Drive, Waynesboro, GA 30830 USA authentic@stl.org

and 9 Holdom Avenue, Bletchley, Milton Keynes, Bucks, MK1 1QR, UK
www.authenticbooks.com

If you would like a copy of our current catalog, contact us at:
1-8MORE-BOOKS
ordersusa@stl.org

The Next Mile[SM]
Short-Term Missions for the Long Haul[SM]

Leader Kit (includes one of each of the following)
ISBN: 1-932805-59-1

Leader Guide
ISBN: 1-932805-60-5

Goer Guide – All-Age Edition
ISBN: 1-932805-62-1

Goer Guide – Youth Edition
ISBN: 1-932805-61-3

Mile Post Devotional, Volume 1
ISBN: 1-932805-63-X

Roadmap
ISBN: 1-932805-64-8

Published in partnership with DELTA Ministries
PO Box 30029
Portland, OR 97294

Cover and interior design: Paul Lewis
Editorial team: Dianne Grudda, Sally Heerwagen, Ron Marrs, Shirley Radford,
Hilary Sarjent, Tom Richards, K.J. Larson

Printed in the United States of America

Contents

Special Thanks

The Next Mile was made possible because of people like Daryl Nuss, Alex Areces, Chris McDaniel, Dianne Grudda, Shirley Radford, Asher and Pam Sarjent, Jeff Binney, Brian Stark, the entire DELTA Ministries staff, and the folks at Authentic Media. Thanks to all of you for your dreaming, studying, writing, and giving so much to this project.

Foreword

Jesus calls us not simply to carry others' burdens for one mile—but to go the next mile as well. In fact, how we walk the second mile will be the proof of our lives as his disciples and will provide the world with a compelling witness to the truth of the gospel.

The quality of a short-term mission experience will be the direct result of the quality of preparation. Its impact on the lives of the hosts and the participants will be determined not simply by what we do when we're there—but what we do when we return. The hardest—and most significant—part of a short-term mission trip begins not when you leave but when you return.

Short-term mission trips are, by design, *short!* As a result, it could well be that the most important aspect of a short-term mission experience is where we typically place the least emphasis—what we do once the trip is over! I wrote a *Short-term Mission Preparation Workbook* (IVP, 2002) as one resource to help mission teams prepare for their return *before* they leave. Now, in *The Next Mile,* we have a comprehensive resource that builds on that workbook and dozens of other excellent resources. Its focus is the integration of our short-term mission experience into our lives once we return.

Millions of dollars each year are being invested in short-term mission experiences. Thousands of hours of hospitality by recipients and hosts are also being invested. God calls us to be good stewards of that investment. *The Next Mile* addresses three aspects of that stewardship: growth in our discipleship, changes in our world view so that we live as responsible global citizens, and on-going partnership with Christians around the world in the years following short-term service.

The Psalmist proclaims, "The earth is the Lord's and the fullness thereof" (Psalm 24:1). May God guide and encourage you to go the next mile into God's world, so that all people might experience the fullness of life right now!

Tim A. Dearborn, Ph.D.
Author of *Short-Term Missions Workbook*
Associate Director for Faith and Development
World Vision International

Preface

Three years ago leaders from nearly 20 ministries gathered at the National Network's Missions Affinity Network Forum (now Youth Missions Network) in San Diego to tackle the challenge of providing effective follow-through for short-term missionaries. The goal was to help short-termers turn their on-field transformational experiences into meaningful, long-term missional lifestyles and commitments. *The Next Mile* resources are part of that collaborative effort.

The Next Mile is a dynamic tool that will help you squeeze the most from your mission experience. As part of a growing legion of young people and adults who are going, serving, and sharing the gospel of Jesus Christ around the world, you now hold in hand a guide that will help you capitalize on the life lessons you will be learning. Furthermore, it will allow you to unpack these experiences in ways that will help you discern God's leading in the future.

I want to thank Brian Heerwagen and his wonderful colleagues at DELTA Ministries who have taken the lead in developing *The Next Mile* materials. They are to be commended for allocating the time and resources to coordinate this effort and make these tools a reality.

As you work your way through this guide and interact with your mentor and friends, I pray that you will see God do immeasurably more in your life than you could ask or imagine. To God be the glory!

Daryl Nuss
Executive Coordinator, Youth Missions Network
National Network of Youth Ministries

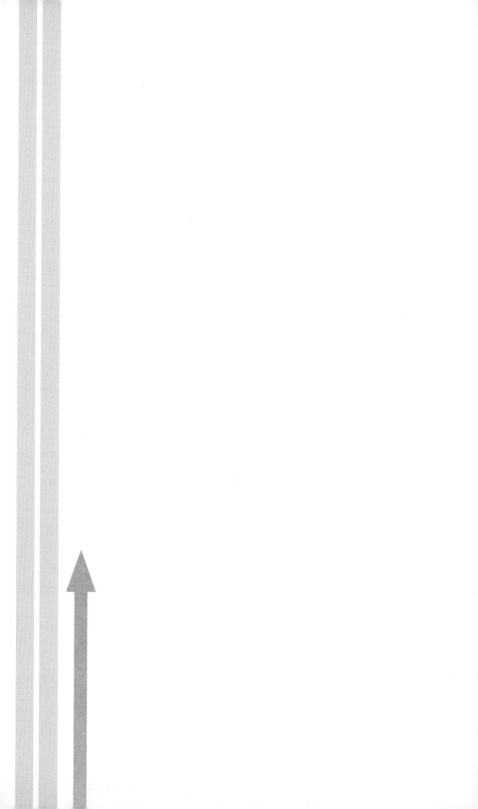

Acknowledgments

We would like to thank the many people who prayed, served, and gave to make the dream of *The Next Mile* a reality. A special acknowledgment goes to the Mission Increase Foundation, Palmcroft Baptist Church, and Washington Heights Church for their belief in the local church and how it can impact global missions through foundational gifts. Their sacrificial giving made the realization of this project possible. May God bless their ministry as they continue to honor him!

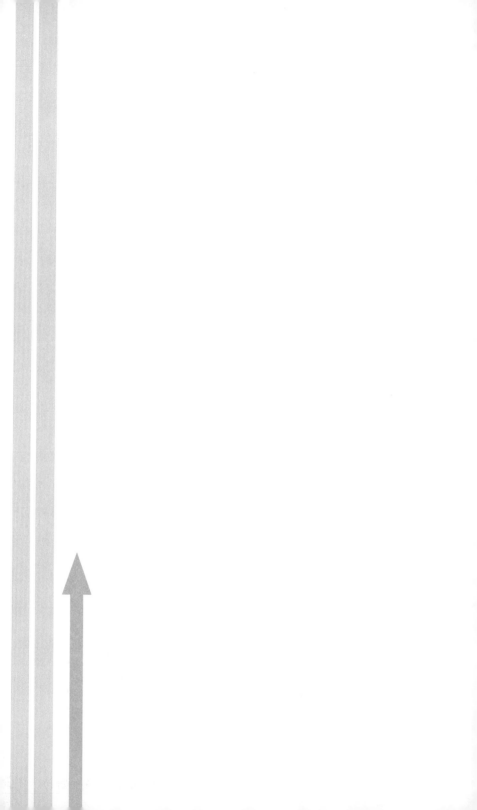

The Journey Starts Here

Short-termers (STMers) come in all ages, sizes, and shapes. And motives for going are different for everyone. In 1965, just over 50,000 people[1] went on a short-term mission (STM). Now over a million go out each year!

Over the years STM organizers have improved in the screening, training, and sending of teams and individuals. However, even though we were learning how to start well, we hadn't figured out how to finish well. So it wasn't surprising after some research to find that the largest percentage of any resource available for short-term ministry is geared to the American short-termer and revolves around *how to prepare* and *how to do* the ministry. When it comes to keeping the flame alive after ministry, there are only paragraphs or chapters here and there.

This is what can be called the "black hole" of short-term missions. While some attempts are made at "debriefing," and organizations are giving a stab at "follow-up," there is little done after the ministry. For most people, life just picks up where it left off: "I did that, now it's back to real life."

However, what about the next mile in the life of a short-termer? Not just the next step (a debriefing meeting) but the weeks, months, and years ahead? Imagine what would happen if you could be intentional about your experiences even after your STM!

AVOIDING THE BLACK HOLE

Follow-up or Follow-through?

"When it comes to the end of our short-term mission, is one meeting enough? Should debriefing be done on the field or back home?" These are common questions for short-term ministry organizers. If you view the mission experience as part of a process, then it will take more than one meeting, and it will require different approaches to stay "dialed in."

Remember learning to throw a football or baseball? The coach told you to "follow through." It's not enough to simply hold the ball correctly or to wind up just right. You need to let your arm continue through the motion. The full throw of your arm and where it is pointing when you are through indicates a lot about where the ball will go and what path it will travel in getting there. How you start and how you finish matters. That's follow-through.

Follow-up implies one event or action. Follow-through communicates the idea of continuing—something that is not bound by time or event. You start with the end in mind.

(Footnotes)
[1] *Maximum Impact Short-Term Mission*, Roger Peterson, Gordon Aeschliman, and R. Wayne Sneed; STEM*Press*, 2003.

1 Mile after Mile

At 17, all Cindy could think about was putting her faith into action on a youth group mission project. She anticipated it. She dreamt about it. She plotted and planned and packed for it. Four weeks later, Cindy returned from her mission trip in rural North Carolina. She felt like a changed person.

The first Sunday back, Cindy blazed with enthusiasm. She spoke to her congregation about the poverty that blighted the area. But she also conveyed the hope she and other "missionaries" brought to the "holler." Cindy shined. She was on fire.

But throughout that fall and winter, I watched Cindy's enthusiastic glow die a slow death. Cindy blamed her growing cynicism on her church, even though it funded her trip. No one heard her plea: "Please, use me for something here! I'm on fire and want to work."

> **PLEASE, USE ME FOR SOMETHING HERE!**

It was a cruel, cruel trick, she said. Churches don't mind teenagers going on missions. But the church doesn't want them to work in the church at home. "This church is spiritually dead," she concluded. "I'm leaving." Cindy quit the church. And she's still looking for a new faith family to give her back the spiritual high she had that summer. She wanted the flame to last forever.

What could've been done to help Cindy's re-entry into her home church? How could her faith community have helped channel her summer enthusiasm into ministry?[1]

Warning: Default Mode

Though few want to admit it, situations like this are not that uncommon. Here's part of how it happened—Cindy did all she could to get ready for her mission, but she gave little or no thought to what should or would come next. Neither did her church or those closest to her. When her trip was done, it was done. But something happened while Cindy was on her mission. She changed.

Often this is how it goes for short-termers: People like Cindy "agonize" over whether or not they should go. Finally, they fill out applications, work hard to raise support, pack their suitcases and head out. They're away from home ... on their "own." It's an experience full of travel, raw adventure, faith, prayer, Bible study, and no showers for 10 days. Then, it's back home. And throughout her experience, the passion to serve Jesus grew. But no one told Cindy what it might be like when she got home. Had she been warned, perhaps she could have made the most of the circumstances and become an inspiration to her church. But instead, it was as though the rug got pulled out from under her.

WARNING

I call this the "default mode" for short-term missions: get organized – go – come back. That's all. It's over. But here is the question that The Next Mile asks:

When is the Short-Term Mission Really Over?

A LIFE–
LONG VIEW

What if God has a longer view of the short-term mission experience? What if he sees the mission trip and all its parts as another element in a life-long discipleship process? In that case, he would care not only about the mission itself, but about all that you go through in preparing for the mission (the mile before) and all that comes after (the next mile), right? He would see the short-term mission as more than a dot on the timeline of your life. It would be a series of events on your spiritual journey—seamlessly blended into all the other events of your life.

Mile after Mile

The following illustration shows the short-term mission as only a self-contained event in a person's life. It starts and it ends. That's all. It's a picture of the default mode for short-term missions. This is what it looks like when you don't do anything more than "just go."

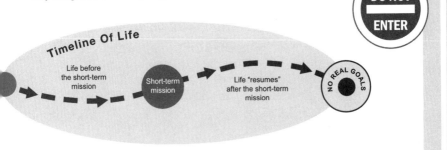

But we believe that God would be thrilled if you were to tackle your short-term mission with the idea that it should span much more time than the mission trip itself. The diagram below illustrates a bigger view of your mission—the idea that you can accept all the events leading up to the mission as a part of the discipleship process, and you can plan for and accept things after the mission as a continuation of what God is doing in your life.

This can be called the "pilgrimage concept." Look at the following chart:

Your Christian life is started on purpose. At some point in time, you decided to follow Jesus. You did it on purpose. In the same way, you must live your Christian life on purpose. Not a series of sprints here and there. But mile after mile after mile.

The apostle Paul gives us a view of why we should do the things we do. He looked "down the road" and he did things on purpose:

> "Do you not know that in a race all the runners run, but only one gets the prize? Run in such a way as to get the prize [*on purpose*]. Everyone who competes in the games goes into strict training [*on purpose*]. They do it to get a crown that will not last; but we do it [*on purpose*] to get a crown that will last forever. Therefore, I do not run like a man running aimlessly [*without purpose*]; I do not fight like a man beating the air [*without purpose*]. No, I beat my body and make it my slave [*on purpose*] so that after I have preached to others, I myself will not be disqualified for the prize."
>
> 1 Corinthians 9:24-27, emphasis added

God cares about your whole life and your whole being. This short-term mission isn't just another trip to the grocery store. It's an important part of what he wants to do in your life. Paul reminds us in Colossians 1:28 about God's long-range purpose and desire for your life: "And we proclaim him, admonishing every man and teaching every man with all wisdom that we may present every man complete in Christ." And in Philippians 1:4-6 Paul writes, "In all my prayers for all of you, I always pray with joy because of your partnership in the gospel from the first day until now, being confident of this, that he who began a good work in you will carry it on to completion until the day of Christ Jesus."

When my friend Leona Bryant discovered she had terminal cancer and only a short time to live, she told me of her radical change in perspective. "The most striking thing that's happened," she said, "is that I find myself totally uninterested in all the conversations about material things. Things used to matter to me, but now I find my thoughts are never on possessions, but always on Christ and people. I consider it a privilege to live each day knowing I'll die soon. What a difference it makes!"

Leona was right. When we view our short today in light of the long tomorrow of eternity, even the little choices we make become tremendously important. After death, we will never have another chance to share Christ with one who can be saved, to give a cup of water to the thirsty, to serve our church. No wonder Scripture commands us, "Set your minds on things above, not on earthly things."

Your life on earth is a dot. From that dot extends a line that goes on for all eternity. Right now you're living in the dot. But what are you living for? Are you living for the dot or for the line? Are you living for earth or for heaven? Are you living for the short today or the long tomorrow? Let's live now in light of eternity.

Randy Alcorn, Eternal Perspective Ministries

(Footnotes)
1 Reprinted by permission, *Group Magazine*, Copyright 1988, Group Publishing, Inc., PO Box 481, Loveland, CO 80539.

2 Well Begun is Half Done

...and how to use The Next Mile Resources

Short-Term Missions for the Long Haul

Everyone agrees that short-term missions should have life-long impact. But believing it and doing something about it are two different things. So what is it that changes a short-term mission from a "mountain-top experience" to a "disciple experience?" Planning—yeah, that's right—planning. One of the keys to being successful for the long-haul is planning everything you need right from the beginning in order to provide a full experience. Get it all on the calendar, have your resources lined up. Work smarter, not harder—don't make it up as you go—otherwise, you will never really finish the race. Remember the race? Run in such a way as to get the prize (the apostle Paul said it that way). So do it all on purpose!

Mary Poppins was hired as the new nanny for two children. In this classic Disney tale, there's a scene where she tells the kids to clean their room. But they don't know where to start! That's when Mary Poppins says, *"Well begun is half done."* It's true! Just starting is half the battle. In The Next Mile you will find what you need to structure your short-term mission. Planning made simple. But you've got to start! Then you're half-way there!

START

AND YOU ARE $1/2$ WAY THERE

I don't think people really understand that a short-term mission is a process. Rather, they tend to focus on the experience in fragmented pieces. Whether it is fundraising, trip logistics, or actual on-site ministry, we don't start the process with the end result in mind. We need to think about what will really make our experience a "success" and how we hope to grow and mature as a person as a result of this missions endeavor. Realizing that a successful short-term mission begins in the planning will greatly impact how we integrate this amazing cross-cultural experience into our lives even years after we made the trip.

Matthew Neigh, Interaction International

NEAT OR MESSY— TAKE THE HIGH ROAD

Neat Freaks and Messies!

Personality and upbringing come into play here. If you are a Neat Freak, having a plan to follow with neat and tidy resources sounds like a dream come true.

But if you're a Messy, the idea of planning, organizing, and following a strategy may leave you looking for a detour, a side road, or a short cut!

The Next Mile is designed for the Neat Freak and for the Messy. Use it page by page, read the book, visit the website, follow it step by step. Or use the headings and pictures to help you find the things you want or the things your team leader told you to find.

In any case, you can't ignore the discipline of actually doing the things that matter. You will need to take this part of your life's journey seriously. Let your attitude be that you want to be different, better, when you come out on the other end of your short-term mission. Don't procrastinate or look for short-cuts. Take the high road!

Use of the Goer Guide

The Goer Guide includes everything you need and is complemented by the additional resources that your team leader has.

Included in the Goer Guide is a Spiritual Journal with daily Bible readings and space to journal, to record thoughts from Scripture, and to write prayer requests. This helpful tool starts 14 days before departure, and continues until a week after returning home. The Spiritual Journal also includes reflection pages appropriate to each stage of ministry. You will find time-appropriate instructions for each portion of the Spiritual Journal in the chapters referring to pre-field, on-field, and post-field in your Goer Guide.

JOURNAL ON PAGE 91

Use of the Mentor Guide

It doesn't matter how old you are. Each and every person, young and old, will be blessed and challenged by having a mentor. It is your responsibility to select a mentor and to deliver the sealed Mentor Guide personally. The following information about roles and qualifications will help you in choosing a mentor. You should get going on this as soon as possible.

What is a mentor?
One of the high school leaders at a church met with the church's elder board, sharing that the young men in the youth group were looking for mentors. After his excellent presentation, one of the older men on the board replied, "But we're not qualified. We don't know how to mentor."

The young man responded, "Just take us to a ball game, pray with us, ask us if we've been in the Word. Be there for us if we need you, do things with us that you normally do. Ask us to help you around your house. Your life is already a teacher to us. Just be yourself. That is the kind of mentor we are looking for."

In other words, it is not required that mentors be Bible scholars, teachers, or even leaders. They just need to live their lives in the presence of another and be intentional about that relationship.

Why have a mentor?
Everyone needs accountability, someone to listen to them, someone to encourage and admonish them. A mentor can come alongside for personal attention and to walk through the transition from life before a short-term mission to a continually-changing life after the ministry.

MENTOR AHEAD

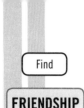

Find

FRIENDSHIP

ACCOUNTABILITY

ENCOURAGEMENT

in your mentor

How do you choose a mentor?

You should seek out someone you respect, who you are willing to spend time with, and who is willing to spend time with you. A mentor should demonstrate the following characteristics:

- A person of prayer
- A person of integrity (if they say they will pray, they mean it)
- A faithful servant in the church
- A person who will commit to at least two months of ministry

What are the roles and responsibilities of a mentor?

The Mentor Packet enclosed with your Goer Guide is sealed and ready to be delivered to your mentor. Inside, there are instructions and ideas for how a mentor can make the most of this mission experience. There are five sections:

- Pray
- Encourage
- Prepare
- Listen
- Report

You can meet at a coffee shop, a park, a ball game, or in the car. You can meet together as many times as you are able. It doesn't matter where or when. All the mentor has to do is follow the simple instructions contained in each section. The Mentor Guide has tools to use during those meetings which require little or no preparation.

Make sure you take some time to discuss the Top 10 issues in Chapter 10 with your Mentor.

Remember, at the heart of mentoring is friendship, accountability, and encouragement. So make sure that you and your mentor have a great time whatever you choose to do!

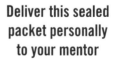

Deliver this sealed packet personally to your mentor

Why Mentoring Matters

You have a hundred things to do. You don't have time for anything else in your schedule. Now you're being asked to be mentored. Why? Because your soul was designed to be mentored just as your body was designed to need food and your heart was designed to be loved.

What is a mentor? A mentor is a "wise and trusted counselor or teacher," someone who listens and guides. It's a new way of saying something ancient and biblical: shepherd. A shepherd provides for, protects, and comforts sheep. You are considered to be like sheep (Psalm 100:3).

How can I say you were designed this way? Because Jesus was designed to be shepherded while he was on earth. He was God Incarnate, full of deity, but also fully man, designed to be cared for, protected, and comforted.

He needed initiatives in his life and ministry. "I tell you the truth, the Son can do nothing by himself; he can do only what he sees his Father doing, because whatever the Father does the Son also does. For the Father loves the Son and shows him all he does. Yes, to your amazement he will show him even greater things than these" (John 5:19-20).

He needed words to speak. "When you have lifted up the Son of Man, then you will know that I am the one I claim to be and that I do nothing on my own but speak just what the Father has taught me" (John 8:28-29).

He was dependent on the Father for his works. "The words I say to you are not just my own. Rather, it is the Father, living in me, who is doing his work" (John 14:10). He needed wisdom, compassion, understanding, and love. Jesus Christ needed his very own relational shepherd—his Father, the Almighty God. In turn, Jesus also shepherded others. He mentored his disciples as they went out on a short-term mission by caring for them, praying for and with them, providing advice, and being there for them when they returned. Jesus debriefed them and helped them gain spiritual wisdom and insight. He did it personally and relationally. (See Luke 9:1-10.)

As you go on your short-term mission, you have the initiatives, words, and works of Jesus through the Holy Spirit present within you. He is your Good Shepherd.

My mentor was Dottie, a former missionary. She spent time with me, showing me what it meant to lay down my life for others. She taught me to go to the Lord in order to respond with kindness when others treated me wrongly.

When I was on a mission as a team co-leader, the Lord used what Dottie taught me, making a night-and-day difference in my experience. My co-leader had never been on a trip before so I was the more experienced one. In a meeting with national leadership, I whispered suggestions in his ear with what I thought was a gentle spirit. He turned to me and said, "What are you, my wife? If you would allow a man to lead, maybe you would be married." Did I want to respond with kindness? No way! I went to the Lord, knowing in my spirit that he wanted me to respond with kindness and even to back off in my leadership role. The Lord brought to memory many things Dottie had taught me, so I remained quiet and responsive to my co-leader. It was the Lord changing me. Although the man never apologized, he did thank me for my response and praised me as a leader. After the mission, Dottie and I discussed the fruit of the Lord in my life from having experienced the power of God to change my response and emotions towards this man. In fact, this man and I are now good friends. I hate to think of the division that could have come if the Lord had not used Dottie ahead of time.

My shepherdess, Dottie (the one who cared for me, taught me, encouraged me, prayed for and with me, and helped me when I returned from my mission), was a direct source from God in his design for me. Eleven years later, she still is.

Terri Vincelette, CultureLink

Mile Posts Devotional

The Mile Posts Devotional is a self-paced Bible study booklet intended for use after the short-term ministry. Each day's reading has been written with short-term missions in mind and is designed to build on training, mentoring, and ministry experiences. These devotions will continue to point you to Scripture and to a lifestyle of ministry wherever you are.

If your team leader has not provided this resource, you can visit **www.thenextmile.org** for ordering information.

Website

Be sure to visit The Next Mile Website for more resources, links to organizations, articles, and mission opportunities.

www.thenextmile.org

3 All for One and One for All

The Three Musketeers used to proclaim, "All for one and one for all!" In today's language we often say, "It's not all about you." Yet in the busyness of life, it is easy for people to get caught up in their very own short-term mission experience and inadvertently leave out all the others surrounding the ministry. The possibilities of all who could be impacted through STM is so vast, it begs us all to consider how to live out, "All for one and one for all."

Participants in Short-Term Mission

Jack walked to the platform and looked out over the crowd. The air crackled with excitement as all the short-term summer mission teams gathered together for pre-field training sessions and a commissioning service. Jack called the team leaders to the front asking them to introduce themselves and their team participants. Each told where their group was from, where they were going, and what they would be doing. It was impressive . . . a group of 10 heading to Lithuania, 14 going to Bolivia, 23 to France . . . and many more. As each group of participants stood during their introduction, Jack said a silent prayer of thanksgiving to the Lord for leading them to take part in a short-term mission.

The last one to be introduced stepped to the mic. "Hi, I'm Sam from New Hope Church in Bakersville. We're going to Kenya to work at an orphanage for six weeks. We have 142 participants."

There was a collective gasp in the auditorium. Wow! 142 participants! Everyone turned to look at the huge group that would be heading to Africa, but only two college kids near the back stood. They grinned and gave a "thumbs up" to their teammate at the mic. Stunned, the crowd turned its gaze to Jack, wondering how he would handle this kid who obviously had just told a whopper. It was all he could do to keep his voice steady, but when Jack spoke, no one could mistake his emotion.

STM IS FOR THE WHOLE CHURCH

Realizing that Sam and his two teammates really got the meaning of short-term mission participants, Jack shook Sam's hand and said, "May the Lord bless you three as you go and all 139 of the other participants in your group as you minister this summer."

What Sam and his teammates understood, and what Jack had been trying to make clear to all of his short-term mission teams, is that "participants" aren't merely those who *go* as STMers, but also those who *send* STMers, and those who *receive* STMers. In the MISTM Grid (Maximum Impact Short-Term Mission) there are three major classifications of short-term mission participants, with six subsets of participants.

MISTM–Grid MAXIMUM IMPACT SHORT-TERM MISSION			PROCESS TRILOGY		
			PRE–field	ON–field	POST–field
PARTICIPANT TRILOGY	SENDERS	Sending Supporters			
		Sending Entity			
	GOER-GUESTS	Goer-Guest Leaders			
		Goer-Guest Followers			
	HOST RECEIVERS	Field Facilitators			
		Intended Receptors			

Senders

Sending Supporters are people who respond to one or more of six means of supporting a short-term missionary. They include prayer supporters, financial supporters, logistical supporters, emotional supporters, communication supporters, and re-entry supporters.

The *Sending Entity* is an organization that is often viewed as the sponsor (e.g., First Church, or ABC Mission Agency.)

Goer-Guests

Goer-Guest leaders are any and all leaders supplied by the sending entities involved. They have certain leadership responsibilities with respect to the short-term mission.

Goer-Guest followers are all the other "goers" on the mission.

Host Receivers

Field Facilitators are individuals and/or their organizations who serve as the on-field liaison for short-term mission arrangements. They are responsible for the receiving-side administration, logistics, field-follow-up, etc.

Intended Receptors are a "targeted" group of people for whom missionaries and sending entities have a burden or a call.

Senders, goers, and receivers are all equal "participants" in short-term mission. Short-term mission can't be done with just one or two of the participant groups. All are mandatory in God's plan.

Roger Peterson, STEM Ministries

SENDER

GOER

RECEIVER

The Next Mile and the MISTM Grid

Each category of the MISTM Grid is important to the overarching success of an STM. Just because The Next Mile is a post-field curriculum and is geared to the goer from a local church doesn't mean that the focus will be on the goer alone, nor will it rest solely on post-field topics.

THERE IS NO SILVER BULLET

Why choose the categories that we did for The Next Mile? To answer that question, you need to hear again the heart of The Next Mile and understand the felt need that led all those involved in the making of The Next Mile to forge ahead with this project.

There Is No "Follow-up Silver Bullet"

No "one-size-fits-all." No "quick-fix." It's going to take effort, intentionality, and a combination of strategies and resources in order to achieve the desired end result.

To Fill the Gap

There are a variety of pre-field and on-field resources available. Yet there is a real lack of resources available for follow-up. The intent of The Next Mile is to provide resources in areas that are lacking, as well as to network all the existing resources together.

As a result, The Next Mile curriculum is providing new resources that can be combined with existing strategies and resources to make full-bodied, short-term missions possible. And the heart of it all is to make missional Christians— radically-committed servants who will shine wherever they live for years and years to come.

The Next Mile includes ideas and resources for pre-field, on-field, and post-field, and provides information relating to:

- Senders (leadership, church, and family)
- Goers (team leaders and team members)
- Receivers (hosts)

For more ideas and resources for each of the categories represented in the MISTM Grid visit www.stmstandards.org or **www.thenextmile.org**.

Find Out How Easy It Can Be!

This is where "working smarter, not harder" starts. It takes some planning and thoughtfulness to involve people in your church or school.The Next Mile provides ideas in this chapter, plus your team leader has a CD with resources on it for your team to use. It's like connect-the-dots or paint-by-numbers! Make good use of the ideas and templates to help you include as many people as you can.

Communication

Communication is key to involving people in the church. People will pray more, give more, and ask more questions if they are a part of what's going on. You will experience a growing momentum in the church for missions as a whole if you are intentional about including all participants. Here are some simple communication suggestions:

 Inserts: There are sample inserts on the CD. Use these ideas to build your own inserts.

Give upbeat announcements from the pulpit, in Sunday school classes, and in small group meetings by a variety of presenters including the senior pastor, team leader, others from the team, even the host missionaries if they are in the area.

 Posters: This a great place to put pictures of the team members, statistics about your destination, job/ministry descriptions, a "thermometer" showing the status of your support and more. There are examples on the CD in PDF format. Copy these ideas or use them to make your own poster creations.

Put up a table or display in the foyer where team members can be each Sunday to answer questions, and to receive donated materials or support. Positioning your table in a prominent place will be a reminder to those who have committed to pray. Those who plan to give donated items or financial support will be more likely to do so if they can count on a stable presence by the STM team.

 PowerPoint presentations may be more appropriate for some churches. You can use the insert and poster concepts on the CD as a check list for things that you should include in PowerPoint programs.

Involving Everyone in the Church

Like Sam, in the story at the beginning of this chapter, you can communicate the all-inclusive nature of your STM. Even though it might be impossible to truly mobilize everyone in your church, you can have a church that is 100 percent behind your short-term mission efforts. One way to be certain that no one feels left out is to offer a lot of options for involvement. It gives people a sense of ownership when they can decide their level of involvement based on their own time, skills, call, and interest.

HAVE A SHORT-TERM MISSION TABLE IN YOUR CHURCH FOYER

SHORT-TERM MISSION NEEDS

YOU

Neither age, gender, financial status, nor physical ability should exclude anyone from being involved. The following section will help spark your imagination on how to include many, many people in the outreach of your team.

Recruit Volunteers
- To organize fundraisers
- To come together with the team to help fold, stuff, address, and mail the support letters
- To host team meetings before and after the mission (move the meetings from home to home instead of defaulting to the church facility)

Promote Resource Donations
Are there items that your team could take that would benefit the ministry where you are going? How about:

- Brand new medical supplies (gauze, bandages, aspirin, etc.)
- Construction paper, scissors, glue for kids
- Small stuffed animals for giving out to children
- Quantities of tracts or Bibles
- Things for the missionaries (peanut butter, Oreos, microwave popcorn—be sure to ask the missionaries what *they* want!)
- Sunday school resources (pictures, flannels, coloring sheets)
- Construction supplies, office supplies

Publish a list for all the church to see, designate the collection location and dates, and wait as the items come in. Sometimes people feel like their financial gift would be too small. But when you provide a way for people to give a tangible gift apart from a financial donation, you've allowed them to become a significant partner in the ministry.

Give Opportunity for Financial Support
- Suggest one-time or monthly financial support through individual gifts, offerings, or sponsorships.
- Let folks hire short-termers in exchange for financial support.
- Set up bottle/can drives, car washes, and other fundraisers.

Recruit Prayer Warriors

- Arrange for prayer during church services before, during, and after ministry by the senior pastor, worship leader, or a delegate from the team.
- Have a sign-up sheet to recruit advocates for team members or aspects of ministry.
- Organize an official prayer meeting once a week for the two months leading up to your mission, during your mission, and for a month following your mission. Have one or all of your team members meet with this prayer group and keep them updated.
- Put prayer announcements in the bulletin each week before, during, and after the ministry.
- Post prayer requests and pictures on a "real time" website managed by someone on your team or in your church.

Host Receiver

Here is an important bit of information about your host receivers. They may be pastors or missionaries, your nationality or another , young or old, cool or not. In any case, you must remember that the host receivers are your authorities. That means that what they say, goes.

They know:

> . . . the culture
> . . . the church or churches with whom you will serve
> . . . the needs of the field
> . . . the size of the team that they can host
> . . . the time and resource limitations
> . . . the vision of the national Christian leadership

In all of your dealings with your host, make it your aim to be a blessing and not a burden. Give more; demand less. *You* be flexible rather than requiring the missionary to flex for you. Take the high road. Be sure to raise enough support so that you do not burden the field financially. You are entering a partnership, one that should be mutual and one that should enable the fulfillment of the long-range goals of the field. So go the extra mile, serve like Jesus served.

INVOLVE EVERYONE, BECAUSE ANYONE CAN

VOLUNTEER

DONATE

SUPPORT

PRAY

NOTES

4 Pre-Field

Some short-termers have been on teams that have had only one meeting before departure. You know . . . it was the meeting where the airline tickets were handed out and there was general discussion about what to bring and when to meet at the airport. No training. No prayer. No mentors. No purpose. Just getting by.

Yet there are so many things that could be covered before ministry; things that have to do with community, character, conflict resolution, and culture; things that give your team more tools, more knowledge, more relationship. In only a few meetings you could cover some important basics along with the logistics that team members and family members always want.

As a team member, do not underestimate the power of praying together, worshiping as a team, and learning together. The Bible talks a lot about relationships, reconciliation, harmony, and love for one another. "They will know we are Christians by our love." Unity comes from quality and quantity time together.

Depending on how your short-term program is organized, there are two kinds of meetings that may be a part of your preparations: (1) pre-field meetings, and (2) training. You must make it a priority to attend all meetings set by your team leader. Here is a brief overview of the things that you might experience in these meetings.

Pre-field meetings
Your team should meet together as often as possible to pray for each other, your church, the ministry, and the mission field. In addition, there are many things that you can include during these meetings. Your team leader has access to templates, sample meeting schedules, and exercises or activities that will make learning fun and memorable. On the next page are some topics that could be included during your pre-field meetings:

- Communication and conflict resolution
- Cross-cultural adaptation
- Language learning
- Testimony preparation, practice, and translators
- Team unity
- Preparation for your ministry role
- Travel logistics and packing tips
- Support discovery
- Goal-setting

Training

It is strongly recommend that you have a formalized training session. This is the time to worship and pray, set down the laws, communicate boundaries, and prepare for specialized projects. It should be biblically-based and cover such categories as:

- Christian conduct
- Character
- Community
- Crossing cultures

Of all the meetings, this is the most important one. Before you ever sign on with a team, make sure you can attend all of the training sessions. Consider this a prerequisite of your going on the short-term mission.

Spiritual Journal – Pre-Ministry

The last section of the Goer Guide includes a Spiritual Journal. The first part begins **14 days before** departure and includes:

**ATTEND
ALL
TRAINING
SESSIONS**

- A Bible passage for each day (focusing on prayer)
- Room to journal about the events of each day
- Reflection pages to be filled out before departure

Take the high road and do all the things required of you before you leave on your STM. You've heard the old saying, "You only get out of something what you put into it." It's true for your STM. The more you put into it at the beginning, the deeper and more impacting the ministry will be for everyone involved.

5 On-Field

Time doesn't make sense on a short-term mission. Days seem to creep by, yet before you know it, the ministry is over. There are cultural stresses, language issues, constant activities, changing team dynamics, new friends, and ever-changing schedules.

It's hard to remember to make time for Bible reading and prayer, for individual reflection, and for unwinding as a team. But if possible, debriefing should take place every day all along the way. Talking and praying through experiences is one of the ways to help you process your journey.

Daily Prayer and Debriefing

Meet together with your team at the beginning and end of each day. Decide right now that it is never an option to miss team meetings. At some of these meetings, you may only have time to close the day in prayer. At other times, your leader will ask questions to help you process the events and emotions of the day. In any case, make a commitment to be a good participant with your team. Your commitment and transparency will be an encouragement and will help others on the team.

On-Field Debriefing Meetings

If you were like most short-termers prior to the mission, you were very excited about your upcoming adventure. Thinking about it was pretty distracting to your work or school respon-

> **TEAM MEETINGS ARE IMPORTANT! BE THERE**

sibilities. You learned about the place you were going to, you thought about the time change, you wondered if you'd have jet lag.

Now it's time to be a little distracted about your trip home. Start thinking about the transition you'll have to make as you return to your own culture and hometown. Some of the things that you should think about are:

- Taking care of unresolved conflict
- Saying good-bye to people and places
- Celebrating all that God has done
- Planning how your team will report home
- Preparing for your return trip and jet lag
- Dealing with re-entry stress

A returnee may experience:

- Unexpected tiredness, confusion, discouragement
- An awareness of habits or behaviors that were second nature before leaving, but seem meaningless or disturbing once home
- Adjustment to role changes that lead to an unsettled feeling
- A change in responsibilities or a change of pace
- An unexpected period of adjustment leading to frustration or anxiety
- A sense of loneliness
- An inability to share the experience and resulting changes
- A negative reaction to the home culture's affluence
- A negative reaction to values presented in the media
- Disillusionment with the abundance in the home culture's church and seeming lack of concern for the world

Adapted from OMF

Reflections Before Going Home

What causes the re-entry time to be difficult for some?

Generally it is because the individual has changed or is changing in attitudes and values, and is coming back to an environment that has not changed in the same way. The deeper these attitude and value changes are in the individual, the more likely that the transition period will be unsettling.

How do people handle this re-entry time?

There are three basic reactions or ways of handling this transition time. You may experience a little of each in the process.

The Assimilators seem to slide right back into the home culture with little or no problem, and appear almost to have forgotten their short-term mission. They seem to have adjusted well, but may have missed out on the greatest growth opportunity. They do not seem to integrate the things they saw, learned, and questioned into a new view of life and the world.

The Alienators seem to reject the home culture. They may be very pessimistic and critical of the home culture, not realizing that they too were a part of it. They may finally succumb to the home culture out of a need to belong somewhere.

The Integrators expect the dissonance they experience, although maybe not in each form that it appears. They are able to identify the changes they have undergone or are still experiencing, and do not demand immediate closure on them. They desire to see their short-term experience have lasting impact on their lives and the lives of others. They grapple with how to integrate the things they saw, learned, and questioned into creative alternative choices.

WHAT WILL YOU BE?

ASSIMILATOR
ALIENATOR
INTEGRATOR

How can I become an Integrator?

The first step is realizing what can happen on re-entry. Most people spend time training for the new culture they will enter, but give little attention to their return. Expectations play a key role in this transition time. If you expect a period of adjustment, you will create the space and time for it and will be less likely to get discouraged while it is happening. Here are a few other helpful hints:

- Get balanced sleep, balanced meals, and balanced exercise. These will help to combat jet lag, tiredness, and apathy that can set in the first few days upon return.

- Spend time thinking through the expectations you had pre-field, on-field, and post-field. Notice any dissonance you may feel now as you return. Notice what values and attitudes are changing.

- Remember to apply the training you received before leaving.

- Debrief with others. Find one other person or a group and ask each other questions like: What did you do? How did you live? What was the easiest? Most difficult? What was funny? What was sad? What did you learn about God? About yourself? About the culture and the people you met? Where do we go from here?

- Re-read your journal. Read one entry every day for several weeks and ask God to remind you of the things he was teaching you then.

- Pray – alone, with a prayer partner, or with a group. Pray for the people you met, the church, each other, the people you want to tell your story to.

- Give yourself a spiritual checkup: Do I feel closer to or more distant from God? What will help my love for Christ grow? Do I need to try something new in my devotions?

- Recall the accomplishments of the short-term mission and develop a list of gifts and strengths that God gave and affirmed. Likewise, make a list of weaknesses and areas where God moved in spite of you.

- Learn how to answer and not despise the question, "How was your trip?"

Adapted from re-entry materials by OMF

Spiritual Journal – On-Field

You have Bible studies, prayer, and journal pages for up to 14 days on the field. Take time daily to be in the Word and to journal your experiences, prayer requests, and answers to prayer.

6 Post-Field

The "default mode" of short-term missions is most glaring during re-entry. The typical feeling is that the "mission is over" and "real life" is about to begin again. While human nature may be prone to compartmentalizing experiences, God is not. He is at work blending one into the next and using all of them as building blocks for growth and impact. Now that you are home again, you have two options:

Drift back to school, job, home, and church without follow-through (the default mode). The thought that your mission trip is "over" and now you must "get back to real life" is going to tempt you to give in to the tyranny of the urgent, and to frantically tackle the business that didn't get done while you were on your STM.

Make a conscious choice to "stay dialed in" and prayerfully and actively do all you can to stay on this spiritual journey. From your earliest involvement, God has been doing something in your life. In fact, he began that work even before a short-term mission was in your thoughts, and his work is going to continue now that you are home.

"In all my prayers for all of you, I always pray with joy because of your partnership in the gospel from the first day until now, being confident of this, that he who began a good work in you will carry it on to completion until the day of Christ Jesus."

Philippians 1:3–6

Short-Term Missions for the Long Haul

Only God knows what this experience has done and will do in your life. You need to do everything you can to hear his voice and to follow wherever he leads. Your commitment to boldly live your Christian faith through outreach, prayer, acts of service, and giving should be ever-growing. It will take a strategy and personal involvement with your team leaders, church, and mentors to keep moving forward in your Christian experience.

Your goal doesn't have to be to go into missions full-time unless that is what God is telling you to do. But your goal does have to be that you will become "missional" in all that you do.

Mission-ary or Mission-al?

I grew up as a missionary kid in the Congo. What a life—full of adventure of all kinds. When my family relocated back to America I struggled with the transition. McDonald's, television, paved roads, and "weird" people could not compete with being a missionary kid. I wanted to go back home.

But the Lord had other plans and we stayed in America. I got used to the traffic and paved roads, and began to appreciate the convenience that comes with living in this country. The more time passed, the more comfortable I became with the status quo. The farther away I got from my childhood experience of adventure and faith, the less I remembered about it.

For many of you who go on a short-term mission, the farther away you get from the experience, the less you are going to remember. If you are going to keep the flame alive and run the next mile with the passion and commitment injected in you from that experience, it's going to require being *missional* not just being a missionary. To be missional is to live life every day with a sense of mission—not just when you're abroad.

Scott and Amy are strong Christians and neighbors of ours. I was leading a team to Africa one summer, so my wife and I decided we were going to invite them to join us. Scott was not a traveler—in fact we joked that he rarely left our city. God removed all the obstacles that might have prevented them from joining us (money, babysitters for kids, etc.), and we had a life-changing trip. I'll never forget what Scott said the night I led

KEEP MOVING

our team in a debriefing session. The question posed to the group was very simple, "What did you learn about God, and what difference is this experience going to make in your life?" Scott stood up and simply stated, "I guess one thing I learned is that God doesn't really care about all the stuff I have in my garage and neither should I. He wants me to use what I have to reach out to other people. I can do that right from home."

What I've come to realize is this: God is not so interested in me being a missionary as he is in me being missional—in living my life for him all day, every day. The height of hypocrisy in many churches is demonstrated when we send people abroad to do something they haven't faithfully practiced here at home. So what did you learn from this short-term mission experience, and what real difference has it made in your life today? Do you just want to be a missionary or do you want to be missional?

John Dix, Mission Pastor
Grace Church, Glendora, California

Post-Field Meetings

The Next Mile has given your team leader some suggestions and resources for post-field meetings. If you committed to attend post-field meetings back when you signed up for your STM, then keep your word. Take the high road and make every effort to be with your team for all the events that you committed to ahead of time.

Spiritual Journal

The spiritual pilgrimage continues after the ministry has come to an end and you have returned home. You have Bible studies and prayer and journal pages for up to seven days after returning from the field. Make time daily to be in the Word and to journal your experiences, prayers, and answers to prayer.

Chapters Seven through Eleven

The rest of The Next Mile Goer Guide includes loads of information that will help you process your experience, tell your story to others, and chart a course for what you should do next. The topics include:

- Returning home
- Reporting home
- Top 10
- Keeping the flame alive
- Goals and evaluations

7 The Turning Point

A Tool Box for Post-Ministry Evaluation

This chapter discusses four important follow-up tools. If your team leader provides any of these resources for you, take them seriously. This post-field season is a critical turning point. How you handle the resources, meetings, and relationships at this juncture will help turn your short-term mission into something for the long haul. Here are the four tools:

An evaluation
Be honest on your evaluation. Prayerfully complete all the questions. Answer them with the goal of strengthening others and strengthening the program in which you were involved.

A goal-setting worksheet
The act of setting goals is daunting for almost everyone. Be sure to set goals that are:

- **S**pecific
- **M**easurable
- **A**ttainable
- **R**ealistic
- **T**arget-dated

Write down the tangible action points that will help you achieve your goals. You can do this exercise even if your team leader doesn't provide you with a form. Here are the categories you can think about:

> USE THE RIGHT TOOLS TO GET THE BEST RESULTS

- Set five (5) one-year goals
- Set three (3) five-year goals
- Set one (1) ten-year goal

Be sure to keep them S.M.A.R.T. and include action points.

A writing assignment

This is a fairly simple assignment. Limit your article to 150 words. Write about how God changed your life or how he used you to change someone else's life. Let your story preach a message rather than using up words to teach a lesson.

A gifts assessment survey

You may have returned home feeling affirmed in what you already knew about yourself. Or the STM may have caused a sense of ambiguity and triggered questions about who you really are or what you should be doing. There are tools available to help you understand your spiritual gifts as well as your skill set and personality. Additional products and links can be found at **www.thenextmile.org**.

Ask your team leader for samples of each of the tools listed above. They are located on The Next Mile Resource CD.

MAKE YOUR GOALS

SPECIFIC
MEASURABLE
ATTAINABLE
REALISTIC
TARGET-DATED

8 Returning Home

The Short-Term Missions Time Warp

If what most experienced short-termers say is true, then you have just experienced more things in a short time than you ever could have if you'd been living the same time span at home. On a short-term mission, there are things happening all day, every day—spiritual, emotional, and cultural things, activities, travel, and relationships—what a whirlwind! The speed of life has been extraordinary!

You may return home feeling like you've been traveling 99 miles per hour. You look at your church, youth group, or small group, and it seems they are traveling at only 12 miles per hour. That is not as much a criticism against the church as it is a commentary on your very full, 24/7, spiritual experience.

It's not until you get home that you usually realize how much you've changed on this accelerated journey. You find out that the change you've experienced runs deep—it's something that happened in your heart and soul. Your goals have changed. The ways you treat people and view things have probably changed, too.

However, the problems you left behind (and maybe even forgot for awhile) are still there. The people at home, living life as usual, have not changed either. In addition, the people you want so much to share with have not been on your trip. In fact, they may never have been on a mission trip at all. They may find it almost impossible to feel and see what you so much want them to understand.

As you merge back into life, it's not uncommon to feel a "distance" between you and others. But, you need to know that integrating the new you with the old ways at home can be done—and done well! This section deals with the common pitfalls you could encounter when you return home and the way people may respond to you. Read these topics with the intent of avoiding the pitfalls and being a blessing to your family, friends, and church as you settle back into life at home.

COMMON PITFALLS
when returning home

Pitfall 1: Too Me-Centered

During research for The Next Mile we had meetings with short-termers and short-term mission organizers. These were done in discussion/survey formats to find out what short-termers feel or experience when they are finished with their mission. This exercise was done to help isolate the top ten issues faced by STMers upon their return. (See chapter 10.)

Something profound came out of the time with one predominately high school/college-age bunch. During the early stages of the discussion this group offered the usual "top of the list" items such as:

> "Nobody really listens when we get home..."

> "It sure seems like the church doesn't really care about me or missions..."

Then one young lady piped up and said, "You know, I think the real problem is that we come back too me-centered. That's the real problem."

And she's right. Typically, short-termers come back with the idea that they deserve to be listened to, that everyone will need to hear the extraordinary stories, and that somehow the church should be thirsty for the kind of life-changing, even church-changing, information they now hold.

But think about this: God gave us two ears and one mouth. That gives us twice the listening power. When you come home, make it your goal to find out how other people are doing. Ask questions about their lives and all that went on during your time away. It's possible that they will ask you questions too. But even if they don't, the Bible says:

COMMON PITFALLS

TOO ME-CENTERED

2

A SELF-RIGHTEOUS ATTITUDE

3

BREAKING ALL THE RULES

4

TALKING INCESSANTLY ABOUT YOUR EXPERIENCE

POST SHORT-TERM MISSION BLUES

REVERSE CULTURE SHOCK

7

UNRESOLVED CONFLICT WITH TEAM MEMBERS

> "Do nothing out of selfish ambition or vain conceit, but in humility consider others better than yourselves. Each of you should look not only to your own interests, but also to the interests of others."
>
> Philippians 2:3-4

Pitfall 2: A Self-Righteous Attitude

I don't think that returning short-termers intend to come across as "holier-than-thou" or as "been-there-done-that" types, but it happens. There are a couple of things at work here.

Holier-Than-Thou. You have been in Christian service 24/7 during your mission trip. That means praying, serving, witnessing, learning—everything you've done has been centered on your Christian faith. Most likely your habits, your worldview, and your conduct have been challenged and have undergone some degree of change. Yet folks at home are in about the same place as when you left. When you reconnect with people, you may experience tension in areas such as movies, shopping, friendships, hospitality, witnessing, time management, and so on. How you respond in those moments will determine how your friends and family view and respond to you. People don't need a sermon on what's appropriate and what's not. Instead, simply let your lifestyle be the teacher.

Been There, Done That. Your experience was far too short and limited for you to be an expert on missions or on the city or country you visited. You will always be learning in your Christian walk, so be careful that what you share with others doesn't imply that you know it all because you've "been there or done that." Qualify what you share with statements like, "In the region we were in …," or, "I know that being a long-term missionary is a lot different than my experience, but…"

Pitfall 3: Breaking All the Rules

The opposite of displaying a self-righteous attitude is breaking the rules or guidelines when your ministry is over. Learning any discipline is hard. When you are free of the rules, the temptation can be to "go back to the way things were." Of course you can let go of some of the rules. Rules about showers, bedtimes, or food may have been instigated for the sake of the community life of your team or organization. But do not ease up on any of the rules that have to do with biblical lifestyle or Christian character.

Pitfall 4: Talking Incessantly about Your Experience

If your short-term mission was as amazing as the ones I've been on, then I know it's hard for you not to talk about it. The mission is the biggest thing in your life. And whenever there is opportunity to talk, you're going to want to talk about your team, the country, adventures, private jokes, and so on. Remember the "two ears one mouth principle?" Find out what is important to other people and express an interest in their lives and experiences too.

TWO EARS, ONE MOUTH
That's twice the listening power!

Pitfall 5: Post-Short-Term-Mission Blues

In many years of working with short-termers, I have yet to meet even one who didn't have some degree of challenge when they returned home. At one end of the spectrum, there are those who suffer little more than jet lag. But at the other end of the spectrum is something I call Post STM Blues. These dark days could be the result of any number of things:

- Missing the camaraderie of your team
- Missing the friends from your ministry location
- Longing for the same spiritual depth that you had while in ministry
- Feeling like you fit better into the host culture than your own
- Being disgusted about flaws in your country's culture
- Returning to difficult family situations at home
- Feeling lost about your future plans

In any case, you need to talk to someone about these feelings. Make an effort to share with your pastor, your mentor, a family member, or a fellow team member. These feelings are not unusual and will be overcome. A tragedy for some who suffer Post STM Blues is that they let these feelings slip into complacency or cynicism that can poison them toward the church or toward Christian fellowship. Some even become angry with God. Don't let that happen to you. Get help immediately and trust God to turn even these feelings into something special.

Pitfall 6: Reverse Culture Shock

How long did you spend preparing for ministry, culture, and language? How many times did you pack (and re-pack) just for practice before your actual departure day? It stands to reason that the more you do to prepare for your journey, the less culture shock there will be.

Many cultures are centered on people, family, and events. It can be disappointing when you come back and find out how much in bondage your own country is to time and money, typically at the expense of the very things that matter most in other cultures—people.

> "...who would have thought that you should spend time preparing for your return in order to minimize the culture shock when you re-enter your own culture?"

Some degree of reverse culture shock is normal and is to be expected. Take your time through the re-entry process. If you pay attention, there are many lessons to be learned. If applied, these things will strengthen your relationships as well as your ministry and work. (Look for more on Reverse Culture Shock in Chapter 10.)

Pitfall 7: Unresolved Conflict with Team Members

"There are only four days left. I can just ride it out and then I won't have to face him any more!" Or, "I can't stand to be with her—after we get home, we won't ever have to do anything else together—so I'm just going to get through these next few days..."

I've heard these and other comments before. I guess it's because people sometimes settle for what's easiest—even if it isn't what's best. Few people like dealing with conflict. They think that maybe it will just go away after the mission is over. But that's not how God says to deal with it. Make every opportunity to keep short accounts while on the mission trip. However, if you bring some unresolved issues home, you need to deal with them.

Be a Peacemaker

Conflict is a part of our daily lives and occurs whether we are on a short-term mission, in a small-group Bible study, or interacting within our own families. The ongoing discipleship process includes learning how to live in harmony with those in the body of Christ. Jesus prayed for our unity in John 17. He said unbelievers in the world would know how much the Father and Son love them by the way believers in Christ treat each other.

For the Christian, conflict can be seen as an opportunity to glorify God, serve others, and grow to be like Christ. If conflict isn't resolved in a wise, biblical manner, the relationship between the two conflicted parties may deteriorate to gossip, slander, or rejection, or lead to broken relationships and long-term damage to the body of Christ.

Resolving conflict is not an option; we are commanded to make peace with God and others. Living in unity is crucial to our testimony as Christians, and although peacemaking is hard work, it is worthwhile as it glorifies God.

> "…conflict is an opportunity, not an accident. Sometimes, our unbiblical reactions to conflict are sinful, rather than the conflict itself."
>
> —Susan Barrett

Resolving conflict begins by asking how one's personal actions and attitudes in a conflict bring glory to God. The next step is to reflect and pray about our own contributions to a conflict before trying to point out someone else's error. Once those two steps have been completed, it is time to go to the other party to attempt to resolve the conflict.

Words can be extremely powerful weapons and the way we use them can make or break any attempt to resolve a conflict (Ephesians 4:29). God helps us address difficult situations through prayer, preparation, and the application of grace.

As you prepare to talk to someone with whom there is a conflict, it helps to remember these guidelines:

- Pray for humility and wisdom.
- Plan words carefully (think of how you would want to be approached).
- Anticipate likely reactions and plan appropriate responses.
- Choose the right time and place (talk in person whenever possible).
- Listen carefully (Proverbs 18:13).
- Speak only to build others up (Ephesians 4:29).
- Ask for feedback from the other person.
- Recognize personal limits; only God can change people (Romans 12:18).

1 Corinthians 6 tells us to take a witness or wise counsel if going by oneself isn't effective.

By God's grace, we can apply peacemaking principles realizing that in God's eyes, success is not a matter of specific results but of faithful, dependent obedience. Our lives as peacemakers bring praise to our Lord and lead others to know his infinite love.

-Bob & Susan Barrett, Peacemakers International

What People Might Say When You Get Home (and how to respond to them)

It's amazing the questions and comments short-termers get when they return to family, friends, and church. Many times I've taught debriefing seminars on this very subject and have received letters saying things like, "I thought my friends and family would be different—that these things would never happen to me. Boy was I wrong! Thanks for giving us a heads-up."

Here are some samples of what you might hear, and in some cases, tips on how you might respond:

"You're back? I didn't know you were gone."

It's hard to keep track of someone else's schedule. In addition, time is relative. So people (whose lives are already full), may lose track of your comings and goings. It's not that they don't care; it's just that they've had other things to focus on.

"How was your vacation?"

Vacation?!? Yeah right! You're probably thinking you need one just to recover from your ministry assignment and travel! Those who see your short-term mission as more of a vacation have probably not been on a short-term mission themselves. And it doesn't help if you were in an extraordinary location! A tendency is to become defensive and "prove" how grueling the ministry was by listing the long hours, the hard labor, and the challenges you faced. Instead, gently turn the attention to the value and impact of the ministry. Just give them some highlights of the amazing things God allowed to happen in people's lives.

**"I'd love to hear all about it. Tell me everything!
Well, I can't talk now, but . . ."**

... and then it seems they never have time to listen. This may be the most common experience for short-termers. It's the day and age we live in. People all around you do care, but they are very short on time and there are so many things about today and tomorrow that distract them from taking a look at things from yesterday. The danger for you is in judging people, believing that because they haven't given you time, they must not care. Instead, just keep trying, waiting, praying, and being patient. There will be the right people at the right time and you'll have opportunities to share.

**"You're back! Great!
We want you to report to the church...**

... and it looks like the first opening is, hmmm ... in about four months. You'll have about five minutes in the evening service and we'd like you to tell us all about your trip." It's important to share with your church or school whenever possible. You may only get the "five minute spot" while other short-termers will be given an entire evening service or a chapel service at school. Be gracious and humbly accept any opportunity you are offered to report on your ministry. Stick to the time limit, and do it for God's glory. In other words, take what you get and do the very best you can.

"I bet it was really hot in the Sahara!"

Gently turn the attention to the value and impact of the ministry. Just give them some highlights of the amazing things that God allowed to happen in people's lives.

That statement would be fine except for the fact that you went to Siberia! To people who haven't been there, Greece, Italy, and Spain can seem like practically the same place. Austria and Australia sound pretty much alike. They're not forgetting or getting mixed up on purpose, it's just that all those places can get confusing. Gently correct errors. Usually these people are genuinely interested; they're just not that great at geography.

**"You've been short-term? Well all I can say about
short-term missions is..."**

... and then they tell you all about the drawbacks of going short-term, dwelling on the high costs, inconvenience to the missionaries, church, and everyone in general, and on bad experiences they've had or heard about. While some of what they have to say may be true, it's typically a very small representation of all that is going on through short-term missions. When you find yourself in conversations like this one, don't make it your goal to change their minds. And don't argue about short-term missions as a whole—it's too big. You can only speak about your own experience and gently turn attention to the impact of the ministry and to what God did in your life or in the lives of others.

A Word about Attention Spans

Here's a common scenario: People ask you to tell them all about your ministry, and they listen pretty well through the first few sentences, or even through your first story. But then you notice that they're beginning to look a little distant or they break in and start to talk about something else.

These people are interested in you and your experiences, but chances are they just can't relate. The trick here is to avoid dumping too much on them all at once. Be prepared with small amounts of information. Tell them one small thing, perhaps an incredible thing you saw God do, or the major thing God taught you. If they're still with you, tell them more, but stop when they show signs that they've reached their threshold.

9 Reporting Home

If you're like most people, public speaking ranks at the top of your "least-favorite-things-to-do" list. But don't skip this chapter. There are two excellent tools here that will make it possible for you to share information that will be meaningful and memorable.

For the moment though, don't think about your report. Don't be nervous or preoccupied by the fear of speaking. Rather, imagine you're sitting in church and about to hear from two short-termers giving a report on their mission. If given the choice, which of the following would you prefer to hear?

John: "Hi. My name is John and I'm from here at this church. They asked me to share about my trip and so, here goes. I'm a little nervous. OK, so as you probably already know, I went on a mission trip to the Philippines and I want to just say thanks for supporting me and for writing letters to me. I had a really, really great time and we did lots of things. It was neat to see the Bible that was translated."

Mark: "I came across an expression of thanks from Grandma Maria in the Philippines. Grandma Maria is 95 years old. When Bible translators first came to her village, she suspected them of coming to steal her language and sell it. She would have nothing to do with them. Today the New Testament is finished in her language. She is a believer and her copy of the New Testament is nearly worn out.

"She says, 'I will never stop reading it. It is my best friend.' If Grandma Maria were here today, she would be the first to thank each of you who supported and prayed for the work of Bible translation.

"Each and every one of you should know that you had a part in God's plan to impact peoples' lives in the Philippines. Thank you."

You would probably listen to *both* John and Mark because you are polite. But you would most likely prefer to listen to Mark because he seems prepared and he is sharing about how people were impacted. Now start to think about your presentation. Wouldn't you rather sound like Mark? It will take preparation, but you can be an effective presenter!

Speaking for Maximum Results

Reporting home effectively is not just something you should *try* to do, but something that you should view as *a necessity*. Whether you're given five minutes or an hour, you must strive to make your presentation informative and memorable. You've probably had to sit through plenty of boring missions presentations. Make up your mind to be different. It matters what you say and how you say it, so work hard at making your presentation the best it can be.

We live in the Age of Information where:

• A weekday edition of the New York Times contains more information than the average person was likely to come across in a lifetime in 17th century England!

• More new information has been produced in the last 30 years than in the previous 5,000 years!

• Information doubles every 18 to 20 months (or less)!

The world is experiencing *"information overload."* We're saturated with information and it's difficult to hear important messages. As a public speaker you must help people understand that what you are saying is important and worth remembering. Make an effort to do more than just talk at people. Bring props, show pictures, do a puppet show, teach a song you learned overseas. Get your audience involved. Engage as much of their brains and as many of their senses as possible. Do whatever it takes to avoid boring people with your presentation. And whatever you do, be enthusiastic and energetic about what you have to report. Do not apologize for the content of your presentation or your degree of preparedness. If you stand up and look bored or apologetic then your audience will soon lose interest.

Remember: Your audience takes their cues from you. If you are enthusiastic and excited about your ministry and communicate it in a clear way, then chances are they will be enthusiastic and excited as well.

Joe Parker, Independent Consultant

You will have more opportunities to present your ministry than you might think. These opportunities will vary in length of time ranging from only a few seconds with one person to an hour-long Sunday evening service. It doesn't take much to be ready for whatever comes your way. One of the most common questions a short-termer is asked upon returning home is "How was your trip?" Some people ask this question mostly as a formality or greeting, while others will really want to know. Whatever the motivation, it is a good idea to have answers prepared for every interest level.

The Sound-Bite
This response is for the person whose interest level is merely a polite greeting. About 15 seconds is good. Think of two complete sentences that encapsulate your experience. You might want to focus on how you saw God work in people's lives or on something you learned.

Interested Conversation
Imagine someone stops you in the foyer between Sunday school and church. The conversation will probably last about five minutes. Have a favorite story or topic ready. Maybe you will also want to be ready to share the most important thing God taught you during your short-term experience.

Public Presentation
These opportunities may come at work, school, or church. Use the two basic methods in this chapter for creating your report. Pray and ask God to anoint your preparation and presentation.

What Not To Do:
Sometimes testimonies do as much harm as good. Those who are unprepared or who do not take the privilege seriously appear awkward and afraid. Those sitting in the audience end up feeling sorry for the speaker and wishing it could be over (as much for the speaker's sake as for their own!) So ...

- Don't wing it.
- Don't ramble.
- Don't go to the platform without knowing how to start and finish your presentation.
- Don't forget to say thank you.
- Don't forget to recognize God's part in the mission.
- Don't end up telling more about sightseeing than you do about the impact on people.

Research shows that about 10% of an audience responds positively to a talk no matter how poorly it's presented, and 10% don't respond regardless of how well it's presented. It's best to minister as effectively as we can to the 80% who can go either way.

Goals When Speaking

How you go about telling your stories is important. Here are some of the goals you should have when preparing to give your report:

- Give God recognition and praise for all he has done.
- Tell how someone's life was impacted and/or how your life was impacted.
- Be a blessing and encouragement to those listening.
- Let your story be a teacher – without you being a preacher.

Steps to a Successful Report

Following are two different approaches to telling your story that will take you step-by-step through preparing and delivering your report. Both are excellent resources, but you may feel you can relate to one better than the other depending on your personality and learning style.

The first resource is called "How to Tell Your Story" from the International Mission Board (IMB) of the Southern Baptist Convention. The second is called "Modules for Memorable Talks" from Wycliffe Bible Translators and Wycliffe Associates.

> *"Go unprepared and you never go alone. Fear is your constant companion."*
>
> Dale Carnegie

How to Tell Your Story   1.
Felicity Burrow, IMB

When telling your story of God's work during your mission project, avoid the temptation to "wing it." Too often "winging it" means that you will:

Speak too long.

Tell stories that interest you but bore your audience.

Overuse "ummm ...," "ah ...," and other "nothing" words that put your listeners to sleep.

If you want people to listen to your stories and care about your mission experience, you need to care enough to prepare.

Who is your audience?
Your presentation will need to be different for a children's Sunday school class than for an older adult Sunday school class or for a collegiate Bible study. Tailor your presentation —stories, pictures, music, etc.—to fit the audience.

What stories will you tell?
Choose stories that show God at work, not just stories about what you learned about yourself (i.e. "I learned I could live without my curling iron for two weeks!").

Choose two or three stories for each presentation that emphasize your point about the work God is doing in the country you visited.

Whenever possible, choose stories that show the host culture and lifestyle in a positive light. If you share, for example, that you had to shake the ants off of your bread at breakfast each morning, most of your audience will only remember the ants and not God's work in your ministry.

How will you tell your stories?
Share your story in the first person (if appropriate), using active and vivid verbs (Ex: "On the road to the village, our truck crawled in and out of potholes the size of small craters" instead of, "Then we went to the village.")

Set a three-to-five minute time limit for each story. Your audience's attention will wander after about four minutes.

Avoid using:

- Vague generalizations about your experience (Ex: "It was so awesome!" versus, "It was awesome when our translator who had been overtly negative about the gospel asked for a Bible.")

- Using the real names of your country of service or of missionaries, national believers/seekers, or villages/towns/cities, if you served in a restricted access country.

- Foreign words that you do not translate.

- Abbreviations of locations (city names, for example) or other items foreign to your audience (names of foods, etc.).

- Names of holidays or other items connected with your host culture/religion which are unfamiliar to your audience. (Ex. If you say, "Ramadan happened while we were there," but you fail to explain that Ramadan is the month of fasting that Muslims observe as a religious ritual, your audience may think that Ramadan is like the state fair.)

- Names of missionaries or nationals who you do not introduce fully to the audience.

What is the Bible truth that you want your audience to remember when they leave your presentation?

Scripture must be the foundation of your presentation. Otherwise you are simply giving a travelogue that any non-believer could give.

Your stories should illustrate truths from the Bible. The Bible is not meant to illustrate your stories (i.e. the Bible is the cake, not just the icing on the cake).

How do you want the audience to respond?
Determine what response you want before you speak. Do you want the audience to leave with only warm-fuzzies about your mission experience, or do you want a more committed response?

Do you want people to pray for your people group? Challenge the audience to pray, and explain how to pray for a people group.

Do you want the audience to consider going on a mission? Challenge them to go, and tell them of opportunities.

Do you want the audience to increase their giving to missions? Challenge them to give up eating a meal at a restaurant or buying a new CD or new clothes, and to put that money toward international missions—possibly toward a ministry need among your people group.

What audio-visual aids will you use?
A picture is worth a thousand words, but some are not worth showing. Select a few high-quality photos or three to five minutes of video about your mission experience.

As with the stories you choose, make sure the pictures or video segment makes your point of what God is doing in your host country. If you show a picture of the tarantula that camped out in your bedroom, your audience will remember only the huge spiders in your host country and not what God is doing there.

PowerPoint is also good for presentations, but not all churches or collegiate groups have the technology to present PowerPoint. Be sure to order the A/V equipment you will need several weeks in advance, especially if the equipment must be ordered from a university A/V department.

How do you get started?
Brainstorm about your memories and make random notes. (Take a plain piece of paper; write the title and the biblical foundation at the top. Now make random notes about your mission experience that fit the foundation you selected.)

From your brainstorming notes, choose two or three stories to tell and write out each story completely, or record them on audiotape.

Time the story to make sure it fits the three-to-five minute time limit.

Write out your entire presentation, so you know what you will say. Have smooth transitions from point to point.

Ask a friend, minister, or professor to listen to your presentation to make sure it is interesting, relevant, and easy for your audience to understand.

Modules for Memorable Talks

2.

Jerry Long, Wycliffe Bible Translators

This approach to speaking will allow you, with minimal training and practice, to give a talk that is memorable, awakens mission vision in the church, and doesn't bore anyone. It is a system of developing brief stories (modules) and organizing them into a talk. We define a module as "a brief story with visual and emotional impact that stands alone and illustrates a single point."

Most of the parables Jesus told can be read in less than a minute. Still, they have made the most revolutionary thoughts of God understandable to the most common of people in hundreds of languages and cultures.

The Two-Minute Rule.
"Brief" means two minutes or less. Why so fussy about the two-minute limit? Admittedly, the discipline is tough to maintain. There is great potential for stress in doing major editorial surgery on a favorite story. There are three important reasons to cut, cut, and cut more on modules:

- Reason One: A module should only illustrate one point.

- Reason Two: Balance. One long story can "out-weigh" the others.

- Reason Three: Attention span. Probably the worst mistake untrained speakers make is to bore their audience by belaboring minor points.

Begin Where the Story Begins.
A good storyteller understands that the audience needs three important pieces of information right up front in a story: when, who, and where. If the speaker gets into the story without giving this information, the audience is distracted by the lack of framework. As a discipline for always getting in the "when, who, and where," make it a practice of putting it in the first ten words of the story. These are called the "Ten Magic Words." Start out with a simple, "During our first term in Africa, my family and I ..." or, "I'll never forget 1974, when in Ecuador, Betty and I ..."

Stop Where the Story Ends.
Don't add morals, applications, explanations, or little sermons to the end of your story. Like a good joke, a good module ends where the story ends, at the punch line. Instead of a punch line,

> The genius of this approach is that when people discover truth for themselves from a parable or story, they own it. They are more likely to believe it, remember it, and apply it when it comes as a discovery rather than a direct admonition or sermon.
>
> -Jerry Long

a module has a "power line." Usually the powerful way to end a story is with the power line and a pause with lock-on eye contact to let the message sink in. Once the listeners discover the message, it's theirs and they will be less likely to forget it.

Know the Opening and Closing Sentence.
An important skill in storytelling is how to get in and out of it. The best way to be sure of that is to memorize the opening ten magic words and the power line.

Learn, but Don't Memorize Modules.
Unless you are a highly trained presenter, when you memorize and recite something it sounds like you are reading it. Other than the opening and closing sentence, don't memorize stories word for word. You will communicate much more warmth if you just know the story well and tell it spontaneously.

Don't Read Modules.
Don't read from a script. When you read, you lose eye contact with your audience, losing warmth and spontaneity.

Don't Write Out Modules Completely
Write out only the ten magic words and the power line. If you need more notes, put the main points of the story on a card and refer to that as needed.

Module Categories
There are 12 categories of modules. The following brief descriptions will help as you plan your modules. Choose three to six of the topics listed, including an Opening and a Closing. Refer to your Spiritual Journey notes for material. [There are samples of all the modules on The Next Mile Resource CD.] Once you have your modules written, organize them according to the needs of your audience. Will you be speaking for five minutes in a morning service? Try this:

- 1 minute—Opening module
- 2 minutes—"Is it worth it all" module
- 2 minutes—Closing module

Do you have 15 minutes? Try a combination like this:

- 1 minute—Opening module
- 2 minutes—Cultural module
- 3 minutes—Action module
- 3 minutes—Nuts and Bolts module
- 2 minutes—Claim/Fulfillment module
- 2 minutes—"Is it worth it all?" module
- 2 minutes—Closing module

The possible combinations are endless. Careful planning on your part can make an inspiring, motivating presentation.

1. Opening.
Usually short and "you-centered" not "me-centered;" the objective is to express appreciation and affirmation to the

> **An audience doesn't care how much you know, until they know how much you care.**
>
> -Claude Bowen

audience. It should be something enjoyable to share. Beware of meaningless words and expressions.

2. Action.

This is a fun story that captures people's attention. It can be a light, action-packed story about travel, kids, pets, food, weather, mishaps. Think of your funniest, scariest, silliest, or most embarrassing moments and relive them in the story. An Action Module can be used just before an opening module because it "sweeps them in."

3. Cultural.

This module portrays a memorable cross-cultural experience that involves customs, traits, language, artifacts, etc. It is important that it shows respect for the people and their culture.

4. Claim/Fulfillment.

Unlike other modules, the Claim is not a story but rather a very brief, direct statement to the audience. It signals a benefit they will gain by listening carefully. For example you might say, "Tonight may well begin a new adventure of faith for every one of you." An audience will respond by thinking, "Wow, if that's true, I'm going to listen to every word this speaker says." Of course you must be able to prove your claim. The Claim may be followed by a brief "Fulfillment" story illustrating how you, or someone else with whom the audience can identify, gained the benefit you are promising. For example, the Fulfillment Module might start out, "Sixteen years ago I was a student sitting where you are today, listening to a missionary talk ..." Then you would briefly portray the impact of that talk on your life.

5. Scriptural.

This module illustrates the truth of a Bible passage. It may portray how Scripture came alive to you because of an incident in your life. Ideally, the application should be so clear from the story that you don't have to spell it out directly.

6. End Result.

This portrays a change in individual lives, families, or communities who were touched by the ministry. This module type should be in every talk. If you only have time for one story, make it an End Result.

7. Nuts and Bolts.

Nuts and Bolts are the basic facts, figures, and details people need to know about your work and about the mission in general.

8. Miracle.

Relive a moment in which God miraculously intervened. Miracle modules portray God's protection, intervention, healing, arranging circumstances, timing, and answers to prayer.

9. Needs Met.

The Needs Met module illustrates how God met a financial need through an obedient person. The person who supplied for the need must be someone to whom the audience can relate. It's best if the story illustrates how the person was blessed or encouraged because he gave. It's also helpful if this kind of statement comes within a story and not at the beginning or end, so that it is not perceived as the primary point.

10. Spiritual Need.

This illustrates the spiritual need of the people we serve. It could portray spiritual bondage, religious practices, substance abuse, or abusive customs. In using Spiritual Need modules, it's important to keep a balance between being truthful and being respectful of cultures. This story must be balanced with what is good about the culture and the people.

11. IIWIA (Is It Worth It All).

Share the moment that you questioned if your work was worth the difficulties, frustrations, delays, sickness, loneliness, or separation from family. Portray how God worked to bring you through, and how he impacted lives through those circumstances.

12. Closing.

Conclude with another expression of gratitude; try using a story to sum up your message. (Just remember not to preach.)

10 The Top 10

Each short-term mission is unique. Culture, personality, team size, leadership, and length of ministry are just a few factors affecting each experience. Despite the incredible variety, it's surprising how many of the feelings and events of returning home can be alike for every short-termer.

Short-termers of all ages have revealed a myriad of issues that have to be processed during re-entry. Through an interactive polling process, it was possible to rank many topics and come up with "The Top 10." The following pages include information and supplemental articles about each topic. You can also visit The Next Mile website for links to videos, books, conferences, and other helpful tools. Go to **www.thenextmile.org**.

The topics are:

1. Reverse Culture Shock
2. Spiritual Warfare
3. Spiritual Disciplines
4. Kingdom Perspective on Life
5. God's Will for My Life
6. Gifts Assessment
7. Marriage and Family
8. Biblical Stewardship
9. Life's Unresolved Hurts and Pains
10. The Impact of Friends

Strike while the iron is hot. You've just seen and experienced things that challenged you and now is the time to act. Nearly all short-termers say their worldview has changed, and their conviction about evangelism and relationships has changed.

The Lord uses experiences like this to reach into your heart and soul. It's OK if you find yourself facing issues that you didn't expect to face. Ask God to guide you. Talk to your mentor, team leader, or other team members as you work through these issues. Here are the topics that other short-termers voted as "The Top 10."

1. The Shock of Returning Home

Reverse Culture Shock
People spend a lot of time preparing for their STM by reading about the culture, studying phrases in a new language, learning about values and new ways of doing things. This research helps adjust their expectations about time and people. However, few STMers remember to think through these same types of issues before returning home. As a result, it's common for short-termers to experience friction upon re-entering their own culture. The more intense the team experience, the more different the culture, and the longer the stay, the more severe this problem can be. Some common reactions are feelings of disgust at the materialism at home, the apparent lack of contentment or gratitude in the American culture, and a frustration at the "sleeping American church."

Short-term missions for the long haul means that you take time to grow and learn through processing these feelings. Remember that no culture is perfect. Be careful that you don't become critical or cynical about either culture. Embrace the good about each one and learn from the mistakes that people make in both places. You may have little power to affect an entire culture or country, but you do have the power to make corrections in your own life.

STM
FOR THE
LONG-HAUL ▶
MEANS ...

Globally Appropriate Lifestyle

There he was ... that big, strong football player sitting all alone in the college dining center, staring into space. I had seen that contemplative expression on his face many times. A year earlier he had returned to campus after his first short-term mission. Since that time he was often found sitting alone, pensive, sometimes crying. I understood his pain from my own experiences in short-term mission and from helping many team members deal with difficult re-entry issues. The deeper and more significant the cross-cultural immersion that occurs in a short-term mission, the more significant the re-entry process becomes. The shock of returning home is a real part of that process.

One of the major issues we face during reverse culture-shock is coming to grips with our materialism. Life seems much simpler during the short-term ministry. Our hosts seem more concerned with people than with their possessions. Tim Dearborn, in *From Mission Tourists to Global Citizens*, raises "8 Great Questions." One of those is "What can I learn about a globally appropriate lifestyle?" How does my experience in a developing nation impact my way of living, especially in my attitudes toward money and possessions?

I was overwhelmed going into a grocery store in the U.S. after spending three weeks in Guatemala on my first short-term mission. We had spent our time working with people of humble means on the construction of their church building. When they went to buy groceries, they only bought a few basic things. They had no choice of brands. And there I was, in an aisle filled with every brand imaginable. Facing a mountain of choices, I felt alienated from my culture. Still, there was pressure to imitate the cultural values surrounding me.

In *Reentry Guide for Short-Term Mission Leaders*, Lisa E. Chinn argues that proactively integrating the good found in both cultures is the best approach to returning home. How is that done when applied to the issue of materialism? How can we live a globally appropriate lifestyle in an American culture of wealth and privilege? Seeing the realities of poverty, malnutrition, lack of basic health care, etc. in underdeveloped nations, we should ask ourselves some hard questions. How do my choices impact giving to my local church, both for local ministries and global efforts? Can I sponsor more children? Can I re-prioritize my budget so that I spend less and give more? What kind of vehicle will I drive? How will I spend my free time? Am I going to the dark places, bringing light and hope to the least and the lost?

The answers to these questions will be different for each of us. For me, it meant giving up my position at Bethel University with its predictable salary to give my full attention to short-term mission at Initiatives International. For that football player, it meant returning to Mexico after graduation to serve as a volunteer staff member at a home for children. What will it mean for you?

David Jensen, Initiatives International

"Proactively integrating the good found in both cultures is the best approach to returning home."
Lisa E. Chinn,
Author of *Re-Entry Guide for Short-Term Mission Leaders*

2. Keeping an Eye on the Battle Field

Spiritual Warfare

It's easy to slip back into life and forget that some very profound things just took place in your life and in the lives of people around you. God used you and your circumstances to make a spiritual difference, and Satan has been fighting against it all along the way. Don't think for a minute that the pressure is off. The Bible says, "Be self-controlled and alert. Your enemy the devil prowls around like a roaring lion looking for someone to devour. Resist him, standing firm in the faith, because you know that your brothers throughout the world are undergoing the same kind of sufferings" (1 Peter 5:8–9).

"For our struggle is not against flesh and blood, but against the rulers, against the authorities, against the powers of this dark world and against the spiritual forces of evil in the heavenly realms" (Ephesians 6:12).

STM FOR THE LONG-HAUL MEANS ... ▶

Short-term missions for the long haul means that you remain alert to the spiritual battle that rages at all times, and you claim God's promises and revel in his strength and protection.

The Devil Has No Landing Pad!

When the subject of spiritual warfare comes up, many tend to deny and diminish its reality; others go way overboard, seeing warfare in almost any circumstance. Let's sort some of this out.

The Bible is abundantly clear that there's a real adversary–Satan–who opposes the purposes of God and his people. Satan perpetrates his influence to accomplish two objectives: to deceive and divert as many people as possible from finding Christ, and to rob the child of God of the enjoyment of salvation and effectiveness in service. But those who see warfare everywhere are, in my opinion, overly simplistic. Satan just doesn't have that much power. While Satan is a real foe, God sovereignly holds the powers of darkness on a long leash.

Every believer, from new babe to old veteran, faces warfare at one time or another. One of the consequences of being a saint in an alien world is that we get some occasional negative attention. We should not be surprised by this "general warfare" against the believer, typically in the form of accusation, fear, discouragement, etc. Beyond this, the pro-active visible Christian worker may experience enemy attacks that are more frequent and intense.

Any Christian worker with a call to witness becomes a light that penetrates the darkness. Holiness of life removes the enemy's handles.

We should heed the challenge to be vessels that are cleansed of sin and healed of life's hurts. Not one of us is perfect, totally "together." But let's be in honest process in these areas. Jesus told his disciples, "The prince of this world is coming, but he has no hold on me" (John 14:30). God has graciously provided us his full armor and the authority of his son to deal with darkness.

James 4:6–10 and Revelation 12:10–12 give us all we need to secure that freedom. Jesus wants you to be able to say with confidence, "The devil has no landing pad in my field of ministry!"

Tom White, Frontline Ministries

3. I'm Done with the Spiritual Stuff, Right?

Spiritual Disciplines

For most people, a short-term mission is an occasion to draw nearer to God, in part because of the expectation and accountability to be in the Word, pray, and trust God in new ways. Being away from all that is familiar, and being placed in challenging circumstances, draws you to God for comfort and strength as well. When you get home, the earlier expectations slip away, the accountability is no longer there, and you're once again in familiar territory.

Short-term missions for the long haul means choosing to remain in the Word and to be a person of prayer. This is truly a discipline because it takes a sheer act of the will to bring "correction or regulation of oneself for the sake of improvement." Don't take the easy road. Be diligent to stay on this spiritual journey, and God will continue to teach and mold you. Instead of a "mountaintop experience" you will enjoy a "new level" in your spiritual growth and find yourself climbing to still greater heights in your relationship with God.

> **STM**
> FOR THE
> LONG-HAUL
> MEANS ...

The Frog in the Pot

Drop a frog into a pot of hot water–it will instantly jump out. Drop a frog into a pot of cold water and it will just swim around. Put that pot on the stove, slowly heat it, and the frog will simply adjust to the changing water temperature until it dies.

We believers are somewhat like the hapless frog. Our surroundings are constantly changing, but often we are oblivious. We just don't seem to get it. In Scripture, God clearly revealed that our three enemies–the world, the flesh, and the devil–will always be at war with the spiritual man or woman that desires to walk with God.

We are exhorted not to be conformed to this world, yet we are pounded with its values, sights, sounds, and philosophies. The media seems determined not to merely report the news, but to subtly shape our thinking. Advertising tries to convince us that happiness and satisfaction come from the "right" kind of shaving cream, cosmetics, clothing, or SUV. Our values are "cooked" by the slowly-increasing temperature of our surroundings.

A short-term mission trip can be a slap-in-the-face wake-up call. It reveals that God is more interested in lost people than he is in our resumes, job potential, or the balance in our savings accounts. We see we have so much compared to those who have so little.

Because our values have been challenged overseas, it's easy to become disillusioned with the church and other believers. Returnees often react to money spent on plush rugs, paved parking lots, padded church pews, and the life-style of their friends compared to needs of kids they saw trying to survive in the garbage dumps of Manila or Mexico City. However, just a few weeks earlier, their thoughts and actions mirrored those of their friends.

How can we live in this world without getting cooked? We must prioritize time with God! It is imperative that before, during, and after a short-term experience we set aside quality time for God's Word and fellowship with him. Every believer acknowledges he or she needs to do this. However, many of us are so busy that we push this discipline aside and sacrifice it on the altar of life and ministry activity. Remember the poor frog? Things seem so cozy, and it's only a degree or two warmer.

The discipline of spending time with God in his Word is a priority before serving him in ministry. Christ retreated to the garden of Gethsemane when he was faced with the biggest decision of all time. He disciplined himself to extended time alone with his Father before he faced the cross!

In your pre-field training, on-field experience, and post-field re-entry, commit yourself to the discipline of spending quality time alone with God. Take advantage of this opportunity to really pray and listen to him. Let the pressures and demands of the world take a back seat to your desire to be tuned in to what God wants for and from you. This is a key to spiritual success. If we are too busy to change, then we better check the water temperature. It's never too late to "jump out" and avoid the fate of the frog that gradually lost its will to change and survive.

Wow, open the window or turn on the AC–I am feeling really warm!

"Remain in me and I will remain in you. No branch can bear fruit by itself; it must remain in the vine. Neither can you bear fruit unless you remain in me. I am the vine and you are the branches. If a man remains in me and I in him, he will bear much fruit; apart from me you can do nothing" (John 15:4-5).

Howard Lisech, Deeper Roots

4. Seeing Things His Way

Kingdom Perspective on Life

On a trip from Italy to the USA, my colleagues and I had "the missing luggage" experience. Six of our seven bags were lost between Amsterdam and Seattle. The seventh was lost between Seattle and Portland. We joined the others in line who had lost luggage in order to fill out papers and describe our bags. You can imagine the swearing, blaming, and demands being hurled at the diligent and innocent counter crew. (By others in the line...not us!) We went home empty-handed that Wednesday night.

While others were angry and impatient, we chose to deal with the situation with understanding, kind words, and grace. You might think that the moral of the story is, "Be kind and God will reward you with the miraculous appearance of your luggage." But that was not God's mind. I won't pretend that I knew his mind at the time. I only knew that he could have had our luggage arrive with us if he wanted to–instead he allowed this circumstance. There's always the thought that, "he's trying to teach *me* something." But this story reveals something about how extraordinary God is. Our behavior that night and the six plus hours at the airport the next day did not go unnoticed. Oddly enough, we were the last ones to get our luggage. It was after 11:00 PM, and we were alone in the office with two airport workers. That's when 25-year-old, 6'5" John asked us about our religion or faith, and we told him we were Christians. Listen to his story. As he held tears back, he described his journey about being a pastor's kid in an abusive church situation, and how his parents were driven from the ministry and later divorced. Since he was 13, he had not set foot in a church. That's when he said it. (A glimpse into God's plans!) He said, "You may be the first real Christians I ever met."

Do you get it? Our luggage wasn't lost by accident. And it wasn't lost in order to teach *me* something. It was so that this young man could see Jesus! This is how God sees circumstances. And it gets better! A few days later, my co-worker went back to collect his payment for a damaged bag. The young lady who was also on shift earlier in the week shared that she had found it difficult to rest since meeting us. She said the impact we had on her co-worker left her wondering what made us different. That day she heard the gospel for the first time!

This situation wasn't about our luggage, any inconvenience, or our rights as paying travelers. That's what other people saw, but not God. He saw two lambs that needed to be rescued. How many times have you been caught up in the details that you can see instead of "riding the wave" and finding out what God has in store for you and other people?

Short-term missions for the long haul means that, "It's not the circumstances that matter; it's what you do with 'em does!" Seek God in the midst of all your circumstances, behave the way Jesus would, and then wait to see what he does!

> It's not the circumstances that matter...it's what you do with 'em that does.

> STM FOR THE LONG-HAUL MEANS ...

God's Got a Plan

I believe the most important thing people need to grapple with is that God has a plan he is working out in history, and we have the opportunity to be a part of it; in fact, it is his desire that we become a part of it. Too many people are looking for "God's plan for my life" as if he has six billion individual plans ... when, in fact, his plan (to bless all the families of the earth through re-establishing his relationship with them through Christ) is universal and unchanging. We cannot "miss God's will" for our lives if we seek his kingdom and righteousness above our own plans. People today are looking more seriously than ever for something bigger than themselves to be a part of; something sure, meaningful, secure, and victorious. God's plan for the earth is what they are seeking. When we give them this lifelong challenge, they are grateful and enthusiastic.

Rebecca Lewis, INSIGHT Program, U.S. Center for World Mission

5. Doing Things His Way

God's Will for My Life

STM usually provides a platform for life-change that brings about a transformation in values and priorities. With that may come a sense that God has something different for you than the track you are currently on. Thus begins the journey to discover God's will.

NOTICE
IF you do these things...THEN you will be able to test and approve what God's will is!

By making careful lifestyle choices, you will better hear his voice. The Bible says:

"Therefore, I urge you, brothers, in view of God's mercy, to offer your bodies as living sacrifices, holy and pleasing to God—this is your spiritual act of worship. Do not conform any longer to the pattern of this world, but be transformed by the renewing of your mind. Then you will be able to test and approve what God's will is—his good, pleasing and perfect will."

Romans 12:1–2

Short-term missions for the long haul means that you earnestly seek God in determining how he will use you here on earth, and that you obey him and put your unwavering trust in him.

STM FOR THE LONG-HAUL MEANS ...

Making Life's Decisions

A life of fruitfulness is the result of making wise life decisions. A major Christian organization observes that the biggest reasons applicants are rejected from their staff are immorality and excessive debt. These pitfalls are the result of unwise decisions.

Even after we determine to be "God-centered" rather than "me-centered," we still face practical "real life" decisions. How can I best prepare for the future? Should I change careers? Should I get additional education? Am I being a good steward of my God-given resources? Am I being a good steward of my time?

There are several significant questions that affect our ability to make wise decisions.

- Am I cultivating a lifestyle that allows me to sense God's leading?

- Have I made Jesus the master of my life? Am I willing to obey his leading?

- Am I living life in the power of the Holy Spirit?

- Is the Bible a vital priority in my life?

- Am I taking time to pray and quietly listen to God?

- Am I putting myself in situations where I can be encouraged and held accountable by other Christians?

If we are consistently growing in these areas, life's "practical decisions" seem easier. The following process may be helpful:

Pray. "If any of you lacks wisdom, he should ask God, who gives generously to all without finding fault, and it will be given to him" (James 1:5). Be honest and specific in your prayers. Pray that God will be honored in your decisions.

Look for evidence of God's leading. In John 15:19, Jesus himself did only what he saw God the Father doing. Where is God already at work? Allow him to open or close doors of opportunity. Be obedient to his leading one step at a time.

Clarify the decision you are making. We can get stuck in an "either/or" decision when there may be other options that we haven't considered.

Get the facts! Sometimes we become anxious because we are making important decisions based on emotions. Once we examine the facts, the decision often becomes obvious.

Seek wise counsel. "Plans fail for lack of counsel, but with many advisers they succeed" (Proverbs 15:22). Get advice from people who have expertise or experience.

Use your "sound mind." "God has not given us the spirit of fear; but of power, and of love and of a sound mind" (2 Timothy 1:7 KJV). A Spirit-controlled Christian should feel free to use his mind to make solid decisions.

Start moving ahead. Once you have reached your best decision, start moving in that direction. Don't let "analysis/paralysis" stop you. It's easier to steer a moving car than a stationary one. Once you are moving in a direction, God can arrange circumstances to move you in the perfect direction.

Think of an upcoming decision you need to make. Get alone and work through the above-mentioned questions and process. Talk with your mentor about what he or she has learned in this area. Finally, remember that God is good and desires to do "immeasurably more than all we ask or imagine" in and through our lives (Ephesians 3:20).

Daryl Nuss, National Network of Youth Ministries

6. Finding Your S.H.A.P.E.

Gifts Assessment

Your short-term mission experience can really challenge what you thought you knew about yourself. Having been asked to do things outside your comfort zone, you may have found that you have more gifts than you knew you had. Now is a good time to revisit your goals, abilities, and gifts. Are you where God wants you to be and doing the things he's gifted you to do?

Short-term missions for the long haul means that you continue to explore all the ways God has gifted you. Apply those gifts in your church, your neighborhood, and the world.

STM
FOR THE
LONG-HAUL
MEANS ...

Finding Your Spiritual SHAPE

You have returned from a life-changing experience. Where do you go from here? Chances are you have been exposed to a new set of ministry challenges and opportunities. As life goes on, many people get stuck serving in areas outside of their effectiveness. Others never realize the joy that comes from understanding their specific calling. How do you discover where God is calling you to serve?

One of the best ways to answer this is to discover your spiritual SHAPE. God has designed you as a one-of-a-kind individual. He has ways for you to contribute to his kingdom that perfectly fit you. Paul explained, "We are God's workmanship, created in Christ Jesus to do good works which God prepared in advance for us to do" (Ephesians 2:10). As God's workmanship, you are specifically crafted to accomplish his plans. A closer look at this verse reveals that God not only created you for good works; he also prepared certain good works for you to do. Therefore, one of the greatest goals of the Christian life is to find out what God created you to do, what he planned in advance for you to accomplish ... and bring them together.

I have discovered that the right tool makes many jobs easier. Ever try clipping a newspaper article with a pair of pliers? Or flipping a hamburger with a stapler? It would be ridiculous. That doesn't mean pliers and staplers aren't wonderful tools for certain jobs. The secret is knowing why a tool was made and then using it for that purpose. In the same way, when you understand what God designed you to do, and as you begin to do it, you will be more fulfilled. The results can be astonishing.

Five Ways to Determine Your Spiritual SHAPE

Use the following five areas forming the acronym, SHAPE, to discover your God-given design for ministry.

S.H.A.P.E.

Spiritual Gifts

Heart

Abilities

Personality

Experience

Spiritual gifts: The New Testament identifies many spiritual gifts that God gives to his children (Romans 12:4–8; 1 Corinthians 12:4–11; Ephesians 4:7–13; and 1 Peter 4:9–11). You probably have two or three prominent spiritual gifts. Here is a list of some common ones:

- Teacher
- Pastor
- Wisdom
- Knowledge
- Giving
- Service
- Mercy
- Evangelism
- Hospitality
- Faith
- Encouragement
- Healing
- Leadership
- Administration

Sometimes we don't recognize our own gifts. A good way to discover them is to ask several godly people who know you well to tell you which ones they see in you. There are also surveys you can take that help identify your gifts (ask your church to recommend one). Most importantly, remember that God will never give you a gift to keep to yourself. His gifts are always intended for you to use to benefit others.

Heart: God places certain passions on a person's heart (Ezra 1:5). Asking yourself what you care about, cry about, and celebrate will help determine the things God has put on your heart.

Abilities: Your abilities are also God-given. The Bible explains that one of the reasons God chose David to be king over Israel was because of his "skill" (Psalm 78:72). What skills do you possess? Make a list. Don't be shy. These abilities are part of the way God has prepared you for effective service.

Personality: Knowing your personality is a great indicator for the type of involvement you should pursue. Paul instructed, "Look well to yourself [to your own personality]" (1 Timothy 4:16 Amplified Bible). Recognizing whether you are reserved or outgoing, task-oriented or people-oriented, a specialist or generalist, will help fine-tune your understanding of God's call upon your life.

Experience: God uses a person's experiences–especially painful ones–to comfort and help other people who face similar difficulties (2 Corinthians 1:3–4). Think about your life experiences, good and bad. How have they shaped you into the person you are today? Where do you have greater compassion and empathy? God may want to use those very areas to serve others.

Your Spiritual Snapshot–Putting it all together

Once you've considered each aspect of your SHAPE, it is time to put it all together. Instead of looking at all the possible ways to influence others that you have listed, focus on the areas of overlap. Think about how some of your spiritual gifts and heart passions might complement your abilities, personality, and experience. Ideally, when you find a ministry where at least four of these elements come together, you can step out with confidence trusting that God has prepared you for this supernatural assignment.

God has shaped you for one-of-a-kind impact. As you discover your divine design, God will lead you into areas of greater satisfaction and impact.

Doug Kyle, Green Valley Church, San Diego

> Apply your God-given gifts to your church, your neigborhood, and the world.

7. Meanwhile, Back at the Ranch...

Marriage and Family

Your STM experience will have an effect on those who are closest to you, and it can impact the way you feel about marriage and family. Some will face the challenge of helping the family process their shared mission experience. Others will be faced with communicating to family members who didn't go on the mission. Because convictions and values have changed so much for the short-termer, it can be particularly difficult when family members don't share the same new insights or changes in lifestyle.

Whether you are single or married, a parent or a child, short-term missions for the long haul means integrating your experiences into life with those closest to you, and finding practical outlets for processing and reconnecting. There are additional resources on your team leader's resource CD and at **www.thenextmile.org**.

STM
FOR THE
LONG-HAUL
MEANS ...

Bringing Your Overseas Experience Back Home

There's no doubt about it. Those who participate in an overseas ministry project come home changed people. Their world has expanded, accompanied by an expanded view of God and the global church he is building. They also return home with a startling perspective on the large disparity that can exist between the realities witnessed overseas and the everyday comforts and privileges afforded those who live in the affluent West.

The new insights you gained on your short-term mission can make it difficult to relate to the family you left behind. They have not had the same experiences nor seen the same realities. If not processed correctly, such a gap in shared experiences can lead to relational tensions. It's easy to lapse into unfair criticism of those who have not been exposed to the new vistas seen by the recently-returned short-term worker. It's a common reaction to view family members as shallow and self-centered, given their lack of appreciation for the expanded perspectives on the world that you have gained.

Here are some ways to minimize such negative tensions and to build positive bridges with the family that is waiting for you back home.

Look for ways to share the experience with your family. Make sure they all know that you want to include them. This could be as simple as bringing back gifts for them. It obviously means sharing stories and photos. Let them know you value having them along for the ride. Don't expect them to get news and reports on your experiences along with everyone else in your world. Give them an inside scoop!

Pray with your family about the ministry and people. In the first few months back home it's important to surround with prayer the people and ministry you left overseas. Involve your family by praying for these new friends around meals and at other special times.

Serve in a project together. One of the best ways to grow a heart for missions with your family is to look for ways to serve together in a ministry project. Look for local or regional projects first. They can provide a much easier point of entry. Increasingly, international organizations are also providing opportunities for families to serve together.

Leave the calling to God. You may have come home with a fresh sense of calling from God to pursue a new avenue of ministry, either here or overseas. Make sure to get wise counsel from your church leaders about the prudence of that emerging sense of call. And be sure to not decide for others in your family what God is now calling them to do. Remember, God will not call a couple into missionary service without making it clear to both of them. Your best course of action may be to share, pray, and wait.

Dave Hall, Emmanuel Faith Community Church, Escondido, CA.

Reconnect, Recommit

As a single adult, the final day of a short-term mission is both the happiest and saddest day of the project for me. I watch team members reuniting with family, waiting for that last one to drive away so I can have one of the features of singlehood I cherish most: true freedom! In some ways, that's self-centered. But that freedom also allows me to move quickly and strategically for the sake of the gospel. Even though that's the happiest day, it's bittersweet. As I open the door to my home I realize I miss that inconvenient but gracious "mission family" that surrounded me for two weeks. This is why I'm especially aware of other single adults who are members of our teams. For that single adult who returns to an empty apartment and empty relationships, post-traumatic-missions-sadness syndrome is very real. I suggest two strategies for single adults who are "re-entering" regular life after a short-term mission: **reconnect and recommit.**

Reconnect: *To friends and family*

After you've been gone even for a short time, you'll have to be purposeful in taking your place in gatherings. Make sure people know you're back in town and back in action.

To team members

For a few weeks, they were your closest friends. But as soon as you got off the airplane, it's like these team members became strangers! There's no reason they shouldn't be among your best friends when you return home. You have experiences that no one else understands. It helps to have someone who can relate when you need to talk or remember. Nurture those friendships.

To church

Once you've returned from the field, be ready to tell your story, but be careful about isolating yourself. It's easy to become the missions nerd! Even though your experience on the field was significant, you're still a member of a dynamic, worshipping community. Your time on the field should make you a better church member. Ask God for ways to strengthen your service through the new perspective you have.

Reconnecting requires that you have something to connect to! That's why recommitting is so important.

Recommit: *To the flexibilities of singlehood*

As a single adult, you have great flexibility for traveling the globe for a missional purpose. You have more flexibility in time, finances, opportunity, and destination than your married friends. Take advantage of this. You can do things now that married people can never do!

To the call of missions

View short-term mission as an opportunity to see God's plan to reach the world. Don't get caught up in the demands of life to the degree that you forget the passion that took you to the field in the first place. Become a voice for missions giving and participation.

To *the call to return*

One of the important principles about "going" is "returning." From the time you walk back through your door with suitcase in hand, start thinking about what to pack for your next journey. In this way, you become a dual citizen, calling two places "home sweet home." Going home will never be the same again!

Mike Jeffries, First Baptist Church, Ft. Lauderdale, FL.

8. Managing Your Stuff

Biblical Stewardship

Venturing into another culture is always eye-opening whether it is inner-city Chicago or a foreign land. You find out how much you have compared to so many others, and you often witness true contentment even in the midst of poverty or other adverse conditions. As you re-evaluate how you spend money and on what things you place value, now is a good time to make significant stewardship decisions. Are you in debt? Then start now with a plan to eliminate that debt. Are you tithing to your local church or giving to missions? Do you support any missionaries? Do you hold tightly to the things that God has entrusted to you, or are you generous with others?

STM
FOR THE
LONG-HAUL
MEANS ...

Short-term missions for the long haul means that you examine your generosity and obedience, and make life-altering decisions about how you handle your finances and worldly possessions. God owns it all, and he wants you to manage your portion well.

Stewardship: Giving as if Every Day Were Your Last

"So then, each of us will give an account of himself to God" (Romans 14:12).

Have you ever spent time imagining the day when you will stand before the most high God and give an account of your life? The thought of standing face-to-face before the Creator who knows our every thought and action brings an overwhelming sense of humility and reverential fear. It creates a healthy sense of urgency and purpose that often seems missing today. This sense of urgency was present in the five virgins in Matthew 25 who were prepared at any moment for the return of the bridegroom.

Romans 14:12 states that we will all give an account of our lives, implying that each of us has been entrusted by God with a unique amount of time, talent, and treasure. We have the awesome privilege of serving as stewards (resource managers) of our King's possessions. On that day when we stand before him, what will matter is how we used his resources to advance his purposes.

While on the mission field, you served 24/7, giving of your time, talent, and treasure to advance God's kingdom. There was an edge, a sense of urgency, to your experience that involved taking risks, pressing forward in situations that seemed impossible, and giving all you had each day for the glory of God. Looking back, you can clearly see how God used you and his body of stewards to provide for every need.

That healthy sense of urgency is missing in every day life for many Christians. In 2004, the Barna Group reported that only nine percent of born-again Christians tithed to a house of worship. Do we give as if each day were our last? Think about it. If you were told that the Lord would take you home today, what might your management of God's resources look like? Would it be different than every other day? Should it be?

Now that you've returned you may be tempted to relax, but don't, because the battle continues back home. Will you dare to trust God to meet all your needs in every day life like you learned to trust him on the field? Wake up each day with the reality that Christ is coming at any moment, and every day give as if it were your last.

Chris McDaniel, DELTA Ministries International

> **"THEREFORE KEEP WATCH, BECAUSE YOU DO NOT KNOW ON WHAT DAY YOUR LORD WILL COME."**
> MATTHEW 24:42

Choosing a God-Honoring Lifestyle

In a probing call to discipleship, Jesus said: "If anyone would come after me, he must deny himself and take up his cross and follow me. For whoever wants to save his life will lose it, but whoever loses his life for me and for the gospel will save it. What good is it for a man to gain the whole world, yet forfeit his soul? Or what can a man give in exchange for his soul?" (Mark 8:34–37).

The number of economic terms in these few verses is striking–save, lose, gain, forfeit, give, and exchange. Every disciple of Jesus is given a radical call as to how he views and handles his money and possessions and every other facet of his life. Whether one has been called to leave his possessions behind for kingdom purposes or to retain ownership for generous and sacrificial kingdom purposes, he must keep in mind that a wrong view of material gain in this world will lure him away from the next. The money and possessions of the present will be of no use on the day his soul is laid bare before his Creator. On that day, money and possessions will be seen as either having facilitated his mission or having blurred or hindered it.

Randy Alcorn, Eternal Perspective Ministries

9. But It Still Hurts...

Life's Unresolved Hurts and Pains

During a short-term mission, it's not uncommon to find yourself at your "stress threshold." This occurs when you have been challenged beyond your normal boundaries, and emotions and experiences find their way out of your heart and back into your thoughts. During this time, you may feel convictions to repair broken relationships, or you may simply be reminded of how much something or someone has hurt you.

It is human nature for people to either ignore offenses and disagreements hoping they will go away, or to fight back with a vengeance. Friendships end, marriages fall apart, and churches split. Whether you are the cause of a hurt or you are involved in circumstances beyond your control, you still have the responsibility to walk as Jesus walked. The Bible is clear about real love, forgiveness, anger, bitterness, and grace. Jesus is the most exceptional example of unconditional love and its effect on all those around him.

STM FOR THE LONG-HAUL MEANS ... Short-term missions for the long haul means taking the high road and acting on these new convictions. It means restoring friendships and seeking forgiveness. God is glorified in reconciliation.

Unresolved Hurts and Pain

Most of us look to the future with optimism. We look forward to realizing our dreams and potential. Yet in the recesses of our soul reside unresolved hurts, conflicts, and sins that quietly become an increasing burden to our life and relationships.

We mistakenly believe that if we take on new relationships, move to a new location, or embrace a new mission or vocation, our unresolved issues or burdens will somehow be left behind. This just isn't true. Unresolved issues will not disappear until we deal with them. In fact, the greatest single reason that Christian workers leave mission assignments is relational conflicts that may stem from unresolved personal issues.

Brent Curtiss and John Eldridge, in *The Sacred Romance*, describe these unresolved issues as arrows to the heart. "At some point, we all face the same decision–what will we do with the Arrows we've known? However they come to us, whether through a loss we experience as abandonment or some deep violation we feel as abuse, their message is always the same: Kill your heart. Divorce it, neglect it, run from it, or indulge it with some anesthetic (our various addictions)."

When any object pierces the body, healing doesn't come until the destructive, infectious object is recognized and removed. Wounds can come in various ways. Some are inflicted on us while we are entirely innocent. Some are self-inflicted as a result of pride or ignorance. Others are the result of guilt from wounds we have inflicted on others.

Now is the time to deal with those murky realities that threaten to destroy us. Life is precious and God's desires for us are too wonderful not to do what is necessary to experience God's best.

Take time to stop and reflect about the inner part of your life. Use pages in your journal to answer the following questions:

- Are there experiences or circumstances that are arrows to your heart? Be specific. Consider that Jesus himself experienced the unjust and painful death on the cross. It may actually be helpful to imagine Jesus coming and pulling out each specific arrow.

- Are there sins in your life that you have never brought into the light? (1 John 1:5–10). Be specific. Claim the promise of 1 John 1:9.

- Are there unresolved conflicts with others for which you need to initiate reconciliation? Are there people you need to forgive or ask for forgiveness? (Colossians 3:13). Be specific.

Once you have acknowledged painful arrows to the heart, confessed unresolved sins, and initiated needed forgiveness, you will be able to serve Christ and others with true joy and freedom. Jesus said, "Come to me, all you who are weary and burdened, and I will give you rest. Take my yoke upon you and learn from me, for I am gentle and humble in heart, and you will find rest for your souls. For my yoke is easy and my burden is light." (Matthew 11:28–30).

Questions for discussion:
- What are you learning about yourself?
- What are you learning about God's involvement in yourlife?
- Are there actions you need to take to make these truths a reality in your life?

Daryl Nuss, National Network of Youth Ministries

10. Friendship for the Ongoing Journey

The Impact of Friends

Ah, the pleasure of spending all that time in the fellowship of others who believe what you believe and who choose to love and serve. If only you could find the same camaraderie at work or school! While you likely won't be able to reproduce the depth of friendship and fellowship found on a short-term team, you can make wise choices about friends. The Bible warns us to not be unequally yoked. If two oxen are yoked together, the two can only be as strong as the weakest ox. To a degree, this applies to friendship in the sense that the wrong friends can drag you down. Yet look at Jesus' example. He spent time with tax collectors and sinners! These two extremes suggest that you must be discerning in how you spend time with friends.

STM FOR THE LONG-HAUL MEANS ...

Short-term missions for the long haul means that you choose friends who will bring out the best in you. Choose to engage in other friendships for the purpose of outreach, but be cautious about how much time you spend with them and what you do with them.

Friends for the Journey

The better part of one's life consists of his friendships.

-Abraham Lincoln

"My command is this: Love each other as I have loved you. Greater love has no one than this, that he lay down his life for his friends" (John 15:12–13).

Sarah went on a short-term mission for two weeks. She made some incredible friends on her project team who encouraged her in her Christian walk. When she returned home she became discontented with her old friends. It was harder to connect with them because her interests and values had changed. They didn't care about the world like she did.

Life's journey is richer, fuller, and stronger when friends are part of the packing list. The question is what kind of friends do you need for the journey?

One of the best models of friendship is Jesus himself.

• Take some time to flip through the gospels and write down the relationships Jesus developed. (Matthew 8:9–12; Luke 7:36–50; Luke 10:1–4; John 6:62–71).

Note that he had a variety of relationships which included non-believers; casual friendships with the 70, close relationships with friends like Mary, Martha, and Lazarus, and the 12 disciples. Then there were Peter, James, and John, his very closest friends.

Jesus' relationships also included a variety of personality types. Look at the differences between Mary and Martha or Peter and Andrew!

- Look up the following verses and write down what kind of relationship Jesus had with each person and his or her personality type. (Mark 10:35–45; Mark 16:9–10; Luke 8:1–3; Luke 9:51–56; Luke 19:1–9; John 1:35–42; John 3; John 4:4–42; John 20:21–29).

- Think through your relationships. Do you have non-believing friends? How about your casual and close friendships? Who are your closest friends? Are there gaps in your relationships? Do you spend all your time with your closest friends and not develop any casual or non-believing friendships?

- Do your friendships include a variety of personality types?

Although Jesus had a variety of relationships, notice that he was careful about choosing those friends that he spent the majority of his time with, namely, his disciples. Read Luke 6:13. Note how Jesus made his decision.

- How have you chosen your closest friends?

Jesus' relationships with his closest friends included sharing everyday experiences, ministering together, providing compassion and comfort, extending truth and forgiveness, and modeling a personal prayer life. Notice one important quality that Jesus displayed with all of his relationships—his desire to serve them. He even mentioned that serving others was his life's mission (Matthew 20:28).

- What kind of friend are you?

- Are you serving your friends?

Friendship is a two-way street. At times we serve others by helping them; at times they help and serve us. Jesus' example keeps us from becoming judgmental, discontented, and impatient with our friends.

In serving them, we find renewed joy and contentment for the journey.

Donna Nuss, Student Venture

> **Be slow in choosing a friend, slower in changing.**
>
> -Benjamin Franklin

> **But every road is rough to me that has no friend to cheer it.**
>
> -Elizabeth Shane

THINK

1. **The Shock of Returning Home**
   What is one thing I learned in my host culture that I can begin to practice in my own life?

2. **Keeping an Eye on the Battle Field**
   What can I do to draw nearer to God and to be less vulnerable to Satan's attacks?

3. **I'm Done With the Spiritual Stuff, Right?**
   Who can help me be consistent in Bible study, prayer and fellowship?

4. **Seeing Things His Way**
   What situation in my life right now do I need to let go of and just "ride the wave" and see what God does?

5. **Doing Things His Way**
   What do I do that clutters my mind and makes it hard to hear God's good, pleasing and perfect will?

6. **Finding Your S.H.A.P.E.**
   What is one thing that God revealed to me about myself and how can I put it to work?

7. **Meanwhile, Back at the Ranch...**
   Rather than make a list of what I think people in my family should be like, write a list of what I should be like for people in my family.

8. **Managing Your Stuff**
   Do I give to affect others, or do I keep all that I can to benefit myself?

9. **But it Still Hurts...**
   Am I holding back from restoring a friendship due to pride or fear?

10. **Friendship for the Ongoing Journey**
    Do each of my friends bring out the best in me?

11 Keeping the Flame Alive

Most people like to play with fire. There's something rewarding about burning long sticks until they're short, melting things, roasting things, or just sitting and watching the flames. But if there is insufficient kindling, the fire will not ignite; and if there is too much wind, the flame will go out. Even so, keeping the flame alive is really not that tricky. By having the right resources and providing enough protection for the flame, it will keep burning (or even grow to a bonfire) and will give off light and warmth that people like to be near. If your experience in missions has allowed God to light a fire under you, or to fan the flame, then add more kindling, add more wood, and make sure you protect the fire from things that will put it out or slow it down.

"You are the light of the world. A city on a hill cannot be hidden. Neither do people light a lamp and put it under a bowl. Instead they put it on its stand, and it gives light to everyone in the house. In the same way, let your light shine before men, that they may see your good deeds and praise your Father in heaven."

Matthew 5:14–16

There are many things you can do to keep the flame alive and to continue to be a L.I.G.H.T. in the world. Here are some practical steps you can take to stay on track spiritually and in ministry.

Live differently. Do you know what will keep your STM from becoming just another mountain-top experience in your life? You. Only you can determine if you will continue the amazing journey of growing nearer to the Lord and of being a blessing to others. For this to happen, you must take on that responsibility and be intentional about your continuing journey.

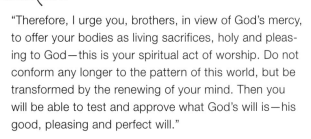

"Therefore, I urge you, brothers, in view of God's mercy, to offer your bodies as living sacrifices, holy and pleasing to God—this is your spiritual act of worship. Do not conform any longer to the pattern of this world, but be transformed by the renewing of your mind. Then you will be able to test and approve what God's will is—his good, pleasing and perfect will."

Romans 12:1–2

You've learned valuable lessons through Scripture and experience. Putting these lessons into practice may cost you something, but consider it in light of God's mercy as a living sacrifice and as an act of worship to him.

Invest in the mission field. You can be a great encouragement to your ministry hosts by keeping in touch with them. Write letters, send birthday cards, pray for them, and join their financial support team.

Guard your mind. The things you allow into your mind have an impact on the way you live. A steady stream of less-than-wholesome television, movies, books, and music will affect your attitude, and will rob you of the joy you have in Christ. Since you might not see any effect at first, it might feel as if you are "getting away with it." However, in the long run you will find that it is like a slow leak. Eventually there will be a blowout, and you will find yourself out of commission spiritually. Remember the old saying, "garbage in, garbage out?" The Bible says:

"Do not be deceived: God cannot be mocked. A man reaps what he sows."

Galatians 6:7

An open mind is good. So is an open window. However, we put a screen on the window to keep the bugs out. Treat your mind like a window and screen what you allow in.

"Finally, brothers, whatever is true, whatever is noble, whatever is right, whatever is pure, whatever is lovely, whatever is admirable—if anything is excellent or praiseworthy—think about such things."

Philippians 4:8

> **"I refuse to be entertained by that which crucified christ."**
>
> **Steve Farrar**

Hide God's Word in your heart. Stay consistent in the study and memorization of the Bible. A diligent effort to know God's Word better will result in a vibrant growing relationship with him. In addition, you can read inspirational missionary biographies that will remind you of the great things God can do with a life that is totally surrendered to him.

Take risks—stay out of your comfort zone! Decide right now that you are not just "at the end of your STM" but actually at the beginning of a new ministry. Plan to live in a way that will continue to stretch you beyond the level of faith you now have. Put your trust in God. Seek to hear his voice and to obey and put into practice all that you have learned. Radical living encourages radical faith!

Do you realize that walking actually requires that you set yourself off balance? As you put one foot in front of the other, you are literally tipping forward–off balance. If you never took the risk of being off balance, you'd be stuck in one place. It's like that in life and faith. The act of "stepping out" and getting a little off balance is the very act that allows you to move forward spiritually. Think about the big steps you took in deciding to go on this short-term mission and look how you've grown! So keep taking risks, following God's wild imagination, and being in the place where you will only succeed if you trust in him and him alone.

Now What?

"Thank you, God. Now I don't know what to do with my life!"

You're back from your short-term mission experience, now what? Is God calling you to return as a long-term missionary? If this question isn't already keeping you up at night, beware–someone will ask it soon. God has shown you what he's doing in the world, and you want to be a part of it. However, packing all your earthly belongings and flying back tomorrow doesn't quite seem right. Even if that day is coming, other factors–school, debt, ministry experience, finding a spouse–may need attention first.

But what if you could significantly build God's kingdom around the world even when you aren't living in another country? Mission work isn't just about those who go. It involves the "Six Practices:" praying, sending, welcoming, going, mobilizing, and learning. How many of these is God leading you to do today? Is he preparing you to focus on others in the future?

Pray: "In the ongoing work of the Kingdom of God, nothing is more important than intercessory prayer" (Richard Foster). Talking to God about the needs of others is vital to growing God's church. Commit to pray for a specific missionary, ministry, or people group (2 Thessalonians 3:1).

Send: Often lost in the "going" of missions is the "sending." Missionaries don't just go overseas: God's people send them. As we so often find throughout the New Testament, the sending-going relationship is one of interdependence: the sender needs the one who goes; the one who goes needs the sender. Intentionally send missionaries through encouragement, logistical support, and finances (Romans 10:15).

Welcome: Every year America hosts over 720,000 international students. Most of them come from the least-reached parts of the world. God can use you in cross-cultural ministry in your city right now. Serve a local English class or international student group while these future leaders live in your neighborhood (1 Kings 8:41–43).

Go: Have you heard glamorous stories of missionary jungle life, extreme risk, suffering, and faith that seem well beyond the capacity of the average Christian? In reality, God doesn't call "super-Christians" to be missionaries; he calls you to live for him in another place. For some, this is just for a few weeks on

6
PRACTICES

PRAY

SEND

WELCOME

GO

MOBILIZE

LEARN

a short-term ministry. But to others, he gives the opportunity for long-term impact through many years of life in another country. Let God place you overseas for as long as he chooses (Luke 4:43).

Mobilize: Picture yourself trying to build a new house. Would your first few days of work be better spent cutting wood or finding committed friends to build with you? Mobilization is drawing others into the work of building God's church. It's more about steadily encouraging people you know than it is about organizing big events. Share the vision God has given you with people you know (Luke 10:2).

Learn: Explore and study what God has stirred up in your heart. Equip yourself to be successful in the mission ministries God gives you. Excellent resources are available in every area of mission involvement. Take a class or read a book to strengthen your ministry.

Work on these practices in small steps. Don't be intimidated by the image of a mobilizer speaking to hundreds of people. Start by sharing one mission story with one friend. Find a community to join you in your exploration. Your teammates may be ideal candidates. Talk and pray often about the Six Practices, how God is leading you, what you're learning, and how to keep charging ahead. Through you, may God's name be made great among every people on earth! (Habakkuk 2:14)

James of OMF International

Outreach and Evangelism

"Preach the Word; be prepared in season and out of season; correct, rebuke and encourage–with great patience and careful instruction."

2 Timothy 4:2

"But in your hearts set apart Christ as Lord. Always be prepared to give an answer to everyone who asks you to give the reason for the hope that you have. But do this with gentleness and respect"

1 Peter 3:15

We have a job to do here on earth. With love, patience, and respect, we are to speak up for what we believe and for who we are in Christ. Hopefully you have new found courage after your short-term mission because you've spent time with people who are courageous and outspoken about their faith. Determine in your heart today that you will keep that fire burning in you and that outreach will become an ever-increasing part of your lifestyle.

When it comes to outreach and evangelism, there are two categories of Christians. The first category is those who are bound up in the activities and pressures of the day. They're always on the backside of the things that they believe "happen to them." They are wrapped up in their performance at work or school, running errands, fixing things, trying to stay in touch with people, but always too busy to do so. To them, life practically drowns out the fact that they are Christians. They are the ones who always say, "Spiritual things just never seem to come up at work."

Then there is the category of Christians whose faith seems to just flow from life's activities. They, too, live a hectic life, but somehow they have a fruitful influence in the lives of people around them. They are the ones who, because of their lifestyle, have people asking them about spiritual things.

There is a fundamental difference. To the first kind of Christian, Christianity has taken a back seat. To them, what they do is more important than their Christian faith. To the second kind of Christian, faith and responsibility to God are always in first place. Higher than a career. Higher than acceptance or fitting in. And higher than any circumstances. Ask yourself the following question by inserting your profession or life activity into the blank:

Am I a _____ who "happens" to be a Christian or a Christian who "happens" to be a _____?

Christians who "happen" to go to school or have a certain job will always place their faith and the responsibility to touch lives for Christ first. Their perspective is that God put them in that school, workplace, or situation because he wanted to affect the lives of those he has entrusted to their care. If you want to live a God-centered life, plan to live your life as a Christian first. If your relationship with Christ is your first concern and you are always looking to become more like him, your spiritual walk will deepen and grow.

This will add strength to your commitment to ministry, and he will use you to influence people all along the way.

To Jerusalem and Beyond

According to the concentric-circle mandate of Acts 1:8, outreach takes us to Jerusalem, Judea, Samaria, and the ends of the earth. "But you will receive power when the Holy Spirit comes on you; and you will be my witnesses in Jerusalem, and in all Judea and Samaria, and to the ends of the earth." Consider these ideas of what outreach to each of these areas might look like.

Reaching Your "Jerusalem." Outreach to the people right around you, often of a similar socioeconomic or cultural/ethnic background.

- As you walk or drive through your neighborhood, pick a specific house, and pray that the people there would come to know Christ.

- Do a prayer walk at your work place. Arrive early and pray over each desk, cubicle, office, or work area.

- Start a book club to discuss popular books and to build relationships with your neighbors or coworkers.

Reaching Your "Judea." Outreach to people in your culture but in the larger region.

> **Preach the gospel at all times, and if necessary, use words.**
>
> St. Francis of Assisi

- Take a university course in philosophy, world religions, or another topic that could open up evangelistic conversations.

- Organize a dinner for people who share your profession; invite a Christian with expertise in that area to speak.

- Get a list of local school principals, and start a regular prayer routine for these key leaders.

Reaching Your "Samaria." Outreach that is cross-cultural but near to home.

- Visit and familiarize yourself with local groups that minister to people who are "cross-cultural" to you (e.g., gangs or HIV/AIDS patients).

- Attend a culturally- or ethnically-distinctive event to understand the cultures in your community.

- Visit leaders of a Muslim mosque, Hindu temple, or Buddhist temple in an effort to understand what other religions believe (and invite them to visit your church).

Reach the "Ends of the Earth." Outreach across your country's borders.

- Pray for an influential world leader to come to know Jesus Christ.

- Call a missionary or international Christian worker simply to offer prayer and encouragement.

- Look ahead and start asking, "Is there someplace in the world where I could use my accumulated experience and skills to serve Christ?"

Paul Borthwick, Development Associates International

Find Ministry in the Church, Community, and World

The continual, joyful giving of yourself for the sake of God's kingdom purposes will help you maintain a close walk with him. Now that you are home, seek out opportunities to serve in the church, community, and world. "For even the Son of Man did not come to be served, but to serve, and to give his life as a ransom for many" (Mark 10:45).

Pray for discernment and eyes to see whatever God might be asking of you. It may be possible to join an existing ministry effort. But if it isn't, don't let a lack of opportunity slow you down—you may need to start something new. Jolaine started a weekly park outreach with a youth ministry team and it lasted for three years. Curtis started an evangelism committee at his church and it is still fruitful today. Darla inspired her church to reach out to the Japanese population in their city. Today there is a Japanese church within their church. Carl left his job and started a company that provides technical support to Christian organizations. As a result, the efforts of each organization are multiplied and there is a much greater impact for the kingdom.

Here are some other possibilities to spur on your creativity:

Ministry in the church

- Help with the youth or children's ministry
- Be a part of the worship team
- Volunteer to be on the missions committee
- Have a ministry of prayer
- Take part in visitation, neighborhood outreach, and evangelism
- Get involved in men's or women's ministry
- Perform acts of service
- Become a Bible study leader or Sunday school teacher

Ministry in the community

- Organize an annual neighborhood clean-up day
- Get involved with local leadership in schools and other public arenas
- Have a cross-cultural outreach to ethnic groups in your city or town

- Lead Bible studies
- Do a park outreach
- Help at a weekly soup kitchen, food bank, or clothes closet for the poor
- Get involved in campus outreach
- Host a kid's club or Vacation Bible School

Ministry in the world

- Adopt a Bibleless people or an unreached people group
- Organize a prayer vigil on behalf of a ministry, mission, country, or church
- Support missionaries
- Organize future STMs
- Begin the process of becoming a mid-term or long-term missionary

Seek God and listen carefully as you choose the things you will be involved in now that you have returned home. Trust him for creativity, availability, and resources to do whatever he calls you to, wherever, and whenever.

Whatever, Wherever, Whenever.

You heard the call of God. It's as real as talking with your friends. God is at work in your life. That's right! Almighty God is communicating with you–everyday-normal-variety-of-person you. But maybe you aren't ordinary. You have opened your life to God. That alone is rather amazing. But even more awesome is that the Almighty is having private conversations with you!

God is consistent. What he is saying to you is probably very close to what he says in the Bible, where he clearly tells you what his will is for you in two general areas:

1. God wants your life, completely and fully. "Understand what the Lord's will is ... be filled with the Spirit" (Ephesians 5:17, 18). "It is God's will that you should be sanctified ... that is holy and honorable" (1 Thessalonians 4:3, 4). "Be perfect ... as your heavenly Father is perfect" (Matthew 5:48).

2. God's will is that every person in the world will come to faith in Christ and spend eternity with God. "The Lord is ... not wanting anyone to perish, but everyone to come to repentance" (2 Peter 3:9). "Your Father in heaven is not willing that any of these ... should be lost" (Matthew18:14). "This is good, and pleases God our Savior, who wants all men to be saved" (1 Timothy 2:3-4).

God is asking you first to be like him (to be holy) and then to expand his kingdom (to share his gospel). He wants you to Do ... Whatever he wants. Go ... Wherever he sends. ...Whenever he calls. Maybe that is what God is talking to you about. So how are you answering when he asks you "Whatever, Wherever, and Whenever?"

You are willing to die for Christ, but are there other things that God is talking to you about? You've quarreled with someone. You know you were partly at fault. God wants you to make it right. Will you? The other day you weren't totally honest. God is asking you to be a person of integrity. Will you? You have something that doesn't belong to you. God is telling you to return it and apologize. Will you? God is talking to you about those DVDs, games, or Internet sights you visit. Will you confess and leave it behind? You and your special friend have been a bit freer with each other than what God, through his Spirit, is telling you is right. Will you listen?

God is calling you to take the next step: having more consistent devotions and prayer, fasting, tithing, sharing Christ with family and friends, doing a short-term mission, going the next mile–taking a longer mission venture, committing to a life of service. Are you willing to say, "God, I am yours from this day forth for Whatever, Wherever, Whenever?"

Glenn Kendall, WorldVenture

Adopt-a-People

There are so many who have not yet heard the good news of Jesus Christ. And there are people groups who do not yet have a Bible in their language. Consider mobilizing your church to adopt an unreached people group or a Bible-less people group. For more information, there are links on The Next Mile website at **www.thenextmile.org**.

Unreached Peoples: The Unfinished Task

"After this I looked and there before me was a great multitude that no one could count, from every nation, tribe, people, and language, standing before the throne and in front of the Lamb." Revelation 7:9 gives us a clear picture of God's heart—he desires none to perish! Jesus commanded his people in what we call the Great Commission (Matthew 24:14) to make disciples of all nations. You may have heard talk that the gospel has been preached in every country. This may or may not be true, but every country is not what the biblical text says. The word nation in the original Greek text of the New Testament is *Ta ethne* from which the word "ethnic" is derived. It has only been in recent centuries that we see more modern nations like the United States as a mix of ethnic groups. For most of history, one's nation was one's nationality or people group. What we call a "nation" in the English language today is more precisely a geopolitical grouping of people; a geographically and politically-defined state.

Throughout history the gospel has spread more easily within people groups. Due to language, cultural barriers, and suspicions between ethnic groups, the gospel often hits a wall outside our own culture. Special efforts need to be made to reach those people groups beyond our own culture.

Let's take a look at a couple of modern-day examples which might help illustrate the point that many countries are really an amalgamation of nations. In the former Yugoslavia there are actually more than five nationalities lumped together; Serbs, Croats, Bosnians, Montenegrins, and Albanians to name a few. Tensions rose among them, resulting in what sadly became well-known as ethnic cleansing. In Iraq we see at least three major nationalities at work, Sunni Arabs, Persian Shiites, and Kurds, with violence erupting among them in a power vacuum. The world is full of these examples.

There are many definitions of "people group," but when boiled down to the simplest definition, a people group is any group that shares a common language and culture that calls us "us" and them "them."

Although the gospel has probably been preached in all geopolitical states, there are still thousands of people groups that have not been reached! These are known as "unreached people groups."

If indeed it is God's heart to reach all nations, it is to these remaining unreached people groups that Christians are commanded to take his message of love and reconciliation in order to fulfill the prophesy of Scripture.

Jesus said, "And this gospel of the kingdom will be preached in the whole world as a testimony to all nations and then the end will come" (Matthew 24:14). God is waiting for his church to take action. Perhaps God is calling you to follow the example of the apostle Paul in taking the gospel to unreached people groups and join him in saying, "It has always been my ambition to preach the gospel where Christ was not known" (Romans 15:20).

Two websites can help you get started. To learn more about unreached peoples and how you might get involved, visit Joshua Project at www.Joshuaproject.net and Caleb Project at www.calebproject.org.

Alex Areces, Independent Consultant

Bibleless Peoples

Powerful, life-changing, incredible, amazing, challenging, humbling ... these words describe your recent mission experience. You may wonder why you have so much and others have so little. Undoubtedly you were humbled by your hosts' outpouring of hospitality. The intensity of your spiritual life soared while God had you outside your comfort zone. Now you're home and things have returned to normal. Or have they? You're thinking differently about "stuff." Your world view has changed, and it's hard to see things the way you used to. It's a bit unsettling. Perhaps you're wondering how, in the midst of the crazy routine of life, you can continue to be involved in God's plan to reach the nations.

There are many ways to stay connected, but one of the simplest and most strategic is to partner with a Bibleless People Group. This type of involvement simply means praying and caring for, learning about and investing in a group of people who do not have the Bible in their language. There are over 2500 such groups in the world.

Have you ever considered what it would be like if you had to worship, pray, or read Scripture in another language?

> "Ty så älskade Gud världen, att han gav sin Son, den enfödde, på dett att var och en, som tror på honom, icke må förgås utan hava evigt liv." John 3:16.

More than 300 million people do not have to imagine that scenario because they do not have access to Scripture in a language they can understand. Having the Bible in the heart language of a people group is foundational to making disciples. Imagine trying to plant a church or train pastors without the Scriptures! Do you see how strategic Bible translation is?

But you aren't a Bible translator ... not anywhere close! Your role in God's plan to reach the nations may be to partner with others who are translators. Your partnership through prayer, financial investment, and practical help can make the difference for an entire people group. So how do you start? Ask God to break your heart for a particular Bibleless People Group. Do the research to find the group God has for you. The Seed Company and/or Wycliffe Bible Translators can help.

In a very simple way you could move from doing missions for two weeks to living a missional lifestyle by investing in an ongoing partnership with a Bibleless People Group. While God has your heart's attention, make the decision that will not only change your life, but the life of an entire people group. There are over 2,500 languages that still need a translation. What if your church (and 2,500 others!) each chose to invest in just one? Then the Church could, indeed, make disciples of all nations. For further information, go to www.theseedcompany.org or www.wycliffe.org

Susie Lipps, Wycliffe / International Impact

12 It Ain't Over Yet!

The Next Mile is not a program, nor is it intended to be a book full of rules, logistics, and outlines. The hope is that you will pour your heart into your short-term mission and make the very most of what God is doing in and through you.

Short-Term Missions for the Long Haul

Your journey began a long time ago, and this short-term mission is just one more leg of that journey. God never wastes any experience in your life. Marriage, graduation, a family crisis, or a short-term mission experience can make you think twice about your values and priorities, and cause you to reconsider how you spend time and manage relationships. It is during these experiences that you make commitments that change the course of your life. Some of the decisions are easily measured, such as choosing a career (wanting to become a doctor and later becoming a doctor), or deciding to move to a new location (determining to move to Philadelphia and later moving to Philadelphia).

While these decisions are fairly concrete and measurable, other decisions are more abstract, and it is not as easy to see them come to fruition. These decisions might include choosing to give more to missions, deciding to share the Lord with co-workers or neighbors, or resolving to spend more time with your family and friends. It's common for short-termers to come home with abstract ideas and hopes like these. As the routine and pressures of life settle in, these measureless goals are usually lost by the wayside.

"You only get out of something that which you put into it." Now that the actual event is over, you can begin to sort out your experiences. Make a commitment today to let God continue his mighty work in you. Use the Bible studies and other resources to keep the flame alive in your life.

You are at the end of one leg of your journey, and the beginning of the next. Enjoy the ride!

Spiritual Journal

Why Journal?

The main desire and ultimate purpose of a short-term mission is to be a catalyst for life-change. This means that what God does in you is as important as what he does through you. You may be going on a mission to make a difference in the world and to change lives, but did you ever think that maybe God wants you to go in order to change *your* life? Of course the people you serve are going to be impacted—but hopefully you will be stretched, challenged, humbled, and broken as you allow God's Spirit, God's people, and God's Word to change you to the very core.

For this reason, using a Spiritual Journal is an important tool—not because it causes life-change, but because it keeps a record. Often we do not remember or are not even aware of how God is changing us. When we are in an intense environment, like a mission project, our senses are opened and the level of spiritual stimuli can be overwhelming. Taking time to chart your growth is an important spiritual discipline.

Remember when you were little and measured yourself on the kitchen wall next to the refrigerator? You didn't notice it at the time, but looking back at the old pencil lines reminded you of how much you'd grown. In the same way, this Spiritual Journal should record marks in areas of your life where God is causing you to grow.

Make good use of this Spiritual Journal. Keep it beyond the length of the mission so you can look back and be reminded of all God has done and continues to do in your life.

How to Journal

Right now your life and weekly commitments are probably fairly familiar and consistent. Developing spiritual discipline in a fixed environment is easier than in a dynamic and unfamiliar setting. That's why it's important for you to start 14 days before your departure using the Pre-Field section. If you are able to be disciplined here, then you will be more likely to be disciplined on the field. Your ministry schedule is going to be packed full of new and interesting experiences. Begin a consistent journaling exercise now as you prepare for service rather than trying to begin during an inconsistent ministry schedule.

- **Step 1:** Choose a time and place that are free of distractions. Morning and/or evening is best—but you will need to find a time that is good for you.

- **Step 2:** Customize the calendar to fit the ministry schedule. Fill in the start date (14 days before departure); enter the dates for the number of days on the field; add seven more days after you return. You or your team leader may choose to add supplementary Scripture readings or other discipleship materials to your daily devotions.

- **Step 3:** Read the daily passage of Scripture and listen to what God is saying to you. Record your thoughts, prayers, and experiences in the journal. Sometimes it is good to share with others what God is teaching, such as at a team debriefing meeting. Other times the lesson may be too personal to reveal.

Helpful Hints about Spiritual Journaling

Be honest – Your journal is between you and the Lord. Utilize this tool to examine your thoughts and feelings. Getting beyond superficial observations will bring a deeper understanding of yourself and God. Follow David's prayer, "Surely you desire truth in the inner parts; you teach me wisdom in the inmost place" (Psalm 51:6).

Be prayerful – Maintain a two-way conversation between you and God. Listen and talk to him as you meet together. Instead of simply reading the Bible, pray through Scripture passages. Rather than building a long list of requests, try writing down some of your prayers as you communicate your heart-feelings with the Lord.

Be creative – Creativity may emerge as you record the discoveries and lessons from your mission. Include pictures, objects, or drawings of special importance. Take along some glue or tape to attach items in your journal. Many times items tell more than words ever could.

Be yourself – Don't worry about how things are worded. This is not an English composition assignment. Just express yourself the best way you can. Your way of keeping a journal is the right way.

How to Use Your Spiritual Journal

The Spiritual Journal includes two key sections:

1. Bible study and journaling
2. Reflections

The Bible study and journaling section is organized chronologically. "Selected Passages for the Journey" outlines the days and topics in the journal. Arranged according to their timeliness during the short-term process, each topic and passage was selected to address a broad spectrum of character and attitude issues encountered in short-term ministry.

- **Pre-Field** – 14 days prior to departure
- **On-Field** – 14 days of ministry
- **Post-Field** – 7 days following your return

The Reflections pages are meant to assist you in assimilating the "big picture" issues during the short-term mission project. These pages are interspersed throughout the Journal for clarifying thoughts, reviewing experiences, and recording long- and short-range goals.

Selected Passages for the Journey

Pre-Field – A Countdown Prior to Departure

14.	A Light to the Nations	Isaiah 49:1–6
13.	Should I Not Be Concerned?	Jonah 4:1–11
12.	A Purpose-Driven Life	Ephesians 2:10
11.	Prepare Your Mind	1 Peter 1:13–16
10.	Alive in Christ	2 Corinthians 4:5–12
9.	Blessed to Be a Blessing	Genesis 12:1–3
8.	Declare His Glory	1 Chronicles 16:23–33
7.	Please, Pray for Me	Ephesians 6:19–20
6.	A Vessel of Honor	2 Timothy 2:20–22
5.	He Will Protect You	Psalm 91
4.	Stand Firm	2 Thessalonians 2:13–17
3.	Strengthened with All Power	Colossians 1:9–14
2.	One Heart and One Mouth	Romans 15:5–6
1.	Greater Things	John 14:12–14

On-Field – While in Ministry

1.	Everything Comes from You	1 Chronicles 29:10–18
2.	Be Alert	1 Peter 5:8–11
3.	One Body – "Parts is Parts"	1 Corinthians 12:12–26
4.	The Greatest Among You	Mark 10:35–45
5.	If It Is the Lord's Will	Acts 18:18–23
6.	True Tolerance	Ephesians 4:1–6
7.	Wise Words	Proverbs 10:19–21; 16:19–24
8.	Follow Your Leader	Hebrews 13:7
9.	Finish His Work	John 4:34–38
10.	Stick with It	Romans 5:3–5
11.	God Chooses the Weak	1 Corinthians 1:26–31
12.	Sheep without a Shepherd	Matthew 9:35–38
13.	Suffering for Glory	Romans 8:18, 28–30
14.	Thank God for Everything	Psalm 95

Post-Field – After You Have Returned Home

1.	Living for His Glory	John 17:1–8
2.	Praying for Protection	John 17:9–19
3.	Continue to Make Him Known	John 17:20–26
4.	Choose Contentment	Hebrews 13:5–6
5.	Number Our Days	Psalm 90
6.	Our Main Ambition	2 Corinthians 5:9–10
7.	Complete in God's Love	1 John 4:16–18

PRE-FIELD—A Countdown to Departure

THE NATIONS | 14

Isaiah 49:1–6

Prayer Requests/Praises

_____

_____

_____

USE THE SECTION AT THE END OF THE SPIRITUAL JOURNAL IF YOU NEED MORE SPACE

SHOULD I NOT BE CONCERNED? | 13

Jonah 4:1–11

Prayer Requests/Praises

_____

_____

_____

A PURPOSE-DRIVEN LIFE | 12

Ephesians 2:10

Prayer Requests/Praises

_____

_____

_____

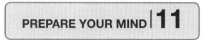

PREPARE YOUR MIND | 11

1 Peter 1:13–16

Prayer Requests/Praises

_____

_____

_____

ALIVE IN CHRIST | 10

2 Corinthians 4:5–12

Prayer Requests/Praises

_____

_____

_____

BLESSED TO BE A BLESSING | 9

Genesis 12:1–3

Prayer Requests/Praises

_____

_____

_____

DECLARE HIS GLORY | 8

1 Chronicles 16:23–33

Prayer Requests/Praises

_____

_____

_____

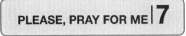

PLEASE, PRAY FOR ME | **7**

Ephesians 6:19–20

Prayer Requests/Praises

_____

_____

_____

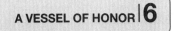

A VESSEL OF HONOR | **6**

2 Timothy 2:20–22

Prayer Requests/Praises

_____

_____

_____

HE WILL PROTECT YOU | **5**

Psalm 91

Prayer Requests/Praises

_____

_____

_____

STAND FIRM | **4**

2 Thessalonians 2:13–17

Prayer Requests/Praises

_____

_____

_____

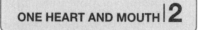

STRENGTHENED WITH ALL POWER | 3

Colossians 1:9–14

Prayer Requests/Praises

_____

_____

_____

ONE HEART AND MOUTH | 2

Romans 15:5–6

Prayer Requests/Praises

_____

_____

_____

GREATER THINGS | 1

John 14:12–14

Prayer Requests/Praises

_____

_____

_____

REFLECTIONS BEFORE YOU DEPART

How has God prepared me for this mission?

_____

What am I hoping to learn about God, myself, the culture?

_____

What area of my life do I think God will need to stretch?

_____

What specific goals do I have for myself? How am I going to achieve these goals?

What specific prayer requests could I share with my prayer partners and family before I go?

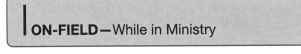

ON-FIELD—While in Ministry

EVERYTHING COMES FROM YOU | 1

1 Chronicles 29:10–18

Prayer Requests/Praises

BE ALERT | 2

1 Peter 5:8–11

Prayer Requests/Praises

ONE BODY — "PARTS IS PARTS" | 3

1 Corinthians 12:12–26

Prayer Requests/Praises

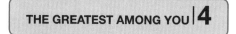

THE GREATEST AMONG YOU | 4

Mark 10:35–45

Prayer Requests/Praises

REFLECTIONS SHORTLY AFTER ARRIVAL

What fears did I exaggerate before my arrival? How have these fears changed?

What are my initial impressions of my team and ministry?

What am I enjoying the most? What factors have made my mission experience positive?

What am I enjoying the least? What factors have made my mission experience difficult?

What are some negative value-judgments and cultural biases I have caught myself thinking?

Is there anything I need to do to make the rest of this ministry better for others and myself?

IF IT IS THE LORD'S WILL | 5

Acts 18:18–23

Prayer Requests/Praises

_____

_____

_____

TRUE TOLERANCE | 6

Ephesians 4:1–6

Prayer Requests/Praises

_____

_____

_____

WISE WORDS | 7

Proverbs 10:19–21; 16:19–24

Prayer Requests/Praises

_____

_____

_____

FOLLOW YOUR LEADER | 8

Hebrews 13:7

Prayer Requests/Praises

_____

_____

_____

FINISH HIS WORK | 9

John 4:34–38

Prayer Requests/Praises

_____

_____

_____

STICK WITH IT | 10

Romans 5:3–5

Prayer Requests/Praises

_____

_____

_____

GOD CHOOSES THE WEAK | 11

1 Corinthians 1:26–31

Prayer Requests/Praises

_____

_____

_____

SHEEP WITHOUT A SHEPHERD | 12

Matthew 9:35–38

Prayer Requests/Praises

_____

_____

_____

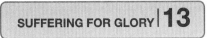

SUFFERING FOR GLORY | 13

Romans 8:18, 28–30

Prayer Requests/Praises

_____

_____

_____

THANK GOD FOR EVERYTHING | 14

Psalm 95

Prayer Requests/Praises

_____

_____

_____

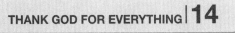

REFLECTIONS BEFORE YOU RETURN HOME

What I appreciated about my team was . . .

_____

What I found difficult about my team was . . .

_____

What I learned the most from my team was . . .

_____

Do I have any unresolved conflict with anyone?
What can I do about it now?

_____

What I will really miss about my team is . . .

_____

When I think of my team I am thankful for . . .

_____

When I think of my teammates, I want to remember:

_____

What I appreciate most about   (Teammate Name)

_____

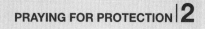

POST-FIELD—After You Have Returned Home

LIVING FOR HIS GLORY | 1

John 17:1–8

Prayer Requests/Praises

_____

_____

_____

PRAYING FOR PROTECTION | 2

John 17:9–19

Prayer Requests/Praises

_____

_____

_____

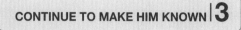

CONTINUE TO MAKE HIM KNOWN | 3

John 17:20–26

Prayer Requests/Praises

_____

_____

_____

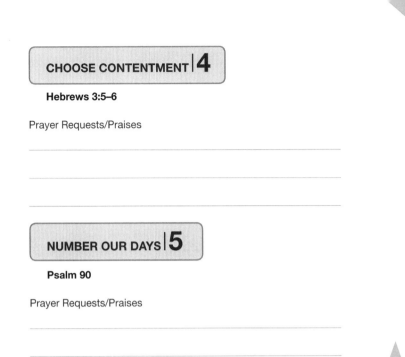

CHOOSE CONTENTMENT | 4

Hebrews 3:5–6

Prayer Requests/Praises

_____

_____

_____

NUMBER OUR DAYS | 5

Psalm 90

Prayer Requests/Praises

_____

_____

_____

OUR MAIN AMBITION | 6

2 Corinthians 5:9–10

Prayer Requests/Praises

_____

_____

_____

COMPLETE IN GOD'S LOVE | 7

1 John 4:16–18

Prayer Requests/Praises

_____

_____

REFLECTIONS AFTER YOU RETURN HOME

When I return home, who will my family and friends meet? What changes have I undergone during my time away? How have I stayed the same? (Consider any shifts in habits, language, ambitions, preferences, values, priorities, etc.)

How have I changed? How am I the same?

Physically / Relationally / Emotionally / Attitudes / Spiritually / Other

_____

What do I anticipate others' responses will be to my changes?

_____

What difficulties do I anticipate I may go through as I return?

_____

What am I most looking forward to about returning home?

_____

Who can I look to for support as I go through the adjustments of returning home?

_____

What other plans can I make for being pro-active in my transition back home? (Consider time for rest, seeing family and friends, reading, journaling, school, work commitments, etc.)

My personal strategy for returning home

The first three days home I want to make sure I . . .

_____

The first week home I want to make sure I . . .

_____

The first month home I want to make sure I . . .

_____

The first three months home I want to make sure I . . .

_____

EXTRA JOURNAL SPACE

Contributors

Alex Areces

Alex is an independent missions consultant who served at Caleb Project for six years. He has previously lived and worked in Asia and Latin America for ten years. He has been part of research teams to unreached people groups and believes that God is currently calling him to use his International Business background to advance the Kingdom in restricted access countries.

Bob & Susan Barrett

www.peacemaker.net

Susan and Bob Barrett are Senior International Representatives for PeaceMaker Ministries. Susan and Bob work both independently and as a team sharing biblical conflict resolution principles and methods. They consult and present workshops to sending structures across the United States and around the world. They act as a facilitators, coaches, and mentors to short and long term mission teams.

Chris McDaniel

www.deltaministries.com

Chris McDaniel, Director of Development for DELTA Ministries International, educates constituents on Biblical stewardship and manages ministry resources according to Biblical principles. Before coming to DELTA Chris handled business, financial, and marketing aspects of other ministries in the Northwest.

Daryl Nuss

www.youthworkers.net

Daryl Nuss is currently the International Networking Coordinator for the National Network of Youth Ministries. He has been on staff with Campus Crusade for Christ and Student Venture and has been directly involved in international mission trips for 13 years. He is also a member of the World Evangelical Alliance's Youth Commission.

Dave Hall

www.efcc.org

Dave serves as World Impact Pastor at Emmanuel Faith Community Church in Escondido, CA. He previously served at Calvary Church in Lancaster, PA and in Spain as a missionary. Also has served on the boards of The Evangelical Alliance Mission (TEAM) and the Alliance for Saturation Church Planting.

David Jensen

www.initiativesinternational.org

David Jensen, Founder and President of Initiatives International, has trained and sent more than 3000 people on short-term mission experiences. He spent 15 years working on college campuses at John Brown University and Bethel University in Minnesota. He is a member of National Short-Term Mission Conference Steering Committee.

Donna Nuss

www.studentventure.com

Donna Nuss is on staff with Student Venture San Diego. She helped pioneer Student Venture's ministry in Moscow, Russia for three years. She helps lead mission projects to Russia annually, served for five years as the Christian Education Director for Green Valley Church in San Diego, and trains/mentors young adults in youth ministry.

Doug Kyle

www.greenvalleychurch.com

Doug Kyle is the Lead Pastor at Green Valley Church in San Diego, California. He received his doctorate from Trinity Evangelical Divinity School in the area of SHAPE-based ministries and has been helping people find their God-given call for over ten years.

Felicity Burrows

www.imb.org

Felicity Burrow is an Associate with International Mission Board (IMB). She is currently the publicity and promotions coordinator and teams coordinator for the Collegiate Mobilization Team. She received a degree in Journalism and Foreign Service from Baylor University and a Master of Divinity degree from Southwestern Baptist Theological Seminary in Fort Worth, TX.

Glenn Kendall

www.worldventure.com

Glenn Kendall is the Africa Ministries Director for WorldVenture (formerly CBInternational). He began serving as the Africa Ministries Director July 1, 1995. During the 13 years he spent in Rwanda, Glenn helped start over 300 churches and groups. While serving as the Personnel Director, he was responsible for recruiting and processing all new WorldVenture missionaries, short-term workers, and summer teams.

Howard & Bonnie Lisech
www.DeeperRoots@aol.com
Howard and Bonnie Lisech began their missionary service in Papua New Guinea. After returning, he served as the director of a short-term ministry for 13 years, mobilizing, training, and sending over 1000 students to 8-week overseas assignments. He is currently serving as a graphic designer for PIONEERS mission agency, and Bonnie has been writing and publishing short-term devotional Bible studies. They also write curriculum and discipleship materials for junior high through adults.

Jerry Long
www.wycliffe.org/theatre
Jerry and Brenda Long have been with Wycliffe Bible Translators for forty years. They first served in Ecuador and Peru. For twenty-five years have spoken for mission events across the continent and have trained missionary speakers around the world. Jerry directs a national touring dinner theatre ministry to raise awareness in churches across the country about Bible translation.

John Dix
www.grace-church.com
John Dix currently serves as an associate pastor at Grace Church of Glendora in the areas of adult ministries and missions. His education includes studies in leadership and missions. He grew up in the Congo where he learned and experienced first hand what oversees ministry is all about. His field experience includes leading teams to Congo, Tanzania, Kenya, Ecuador, Romania, China, and the Czech Republic.

Joseph Parker
jparker@elic.org
Joseph has done non-profit management work for 39 years—the past 28 with Christian organizations, assisting in funds development, strategic planning and board effectiveness. Public speaking is a specialty, especially in preparing leaders for powerful presentations, highlighting vision and mission. Served more than sixty ministries of all sizes since 1977 whose call is to advance the cause of Christ.

Matthew Neigh
www.interactionintl.org
Matthew Neigh, Executive Director of Interaction International, has traveled to over 47 countries conducting seminars, training and consulting for the expatriate community. He also serves as an associate with Global Associates. He currently serves as the President of the Board of Directors of Families In Global Transition, Inc. (FIGT), and sits on the Board of Directors of other international non-profit organization.

Mike Jeffries
www.fbcnet.com

Mike Jeffries leads the missions mobilization programs at the 12,000-member First Baptist Church of Fort Lauderdale. Mike's passion is seeing believers equipped and emboldened for cross-cultural ministry. He has led short-term teams for more than a decade, traveling to dozens of nations. His primary focus nations have been Russia and Nicaragua and he's led twenty-one teams to each of these countries.

OMF International
www.us.omf.org

OMF International (started as the China Inland Mission) is a diverse fellowship of 1,300 Christians from 30 nationalities with a passion for proclaiming the glory of Jesus Christ among East Asia's peoples. Our vision is to see an indigenous, biblical church movement in each people group of East Asia, evangelizing their own people and reaching out in mission to others. OMF uses a wide variety of creative short-term and long-term ministries to share the gospel to East Asia's unreached peoples.

Paul Borthwick
www.daintl.org

Paul Borthwick serves as Senior Consultant for Development Associates International, a ministry dedicated in leadership development in the under-resourced world. Paul's ministry focuses on mobilizing others for cross-cultural ministry, encouraging the ongoing growth of older leaders, and motivating the development of younger leaders. He is the author of 14 books.

Randy Alcorn
www.epm.org

He is the founder and director of Eternal Perspective Ministries, a non-profit organization whose goal is to encourage an eternal perspective through a teaching and reaching ministry, with emphasis on missions and prolife work. EPM is dedicated to teaching biblical truth and drawing attention to the needy and how to help them. EPM exists to meet the needs of the unreached, unfed, unborn, uneducated, unreconciled, and unsupported people around the world.

Rebecca Lewis
www.uscwm.org/insight

Rebecca Lewis has spent 15 years working with Frontiers in ministry to Muslim women and currently has developed a 32 credit college-level training program studying the sweep of God's work throughout history called INSIGHT (INtensive Study of Global History and Theology).

Rev. Roger Peterson
www.stemmin.org
Rev. Roger Peterson is the Founder and Executive Director of STEM Int'l, an international short-term mission organization. He has administered, organized, trained, and/or led more than 300 short-term mission teams, representing more than 5,000 short-termers since 1980. Peterson also chairs the Board of Directors for AESTM (Alliance for Excellence in Short-Term Mission). AESTM is a Christian nonprofit holding corporation for FSTML, NSTMC, and SOE.

Susie Lipps
www.internationalimpact.com
Susie Lipps is an MK from Central America. She has been a member of Wycliffe for 22 years and is currently serving as the President of International Impact. Her passion is to see this global generation fulfilling their role in God's plan to reach the nations. Susie is married to an incredible guy named Bob and has three outstanding, adult children Jonathan, David and Rachel.

Terri L. (Hughes) Vincelette
Culture Link Inc.
Terri is a trainer and short-term consultant with CultureLink, Inc. CultureLink provides seminars for short-term team leaders. Terri led teams to over 20 countries. She was on staff with SEND International for 10 years and developed their short-term missions program. She is married to Gary Vincelette and serves with him in Global Outreach for Christian Fellowship Church in Evansville, Indiana.

Tom White
www.flministries.org
Founder and President of Frontline Ministries, Tom White conducts an international ministry developing citywide prayer movements, and teaching in the areas of spiritual warfare, intercession, and strategic city reaching. Currently he serves as Convener of the North American City Impact Roundtable, and leads the Transformational Prayer Community Facilitation Group for the Transform World movement.

Tim Dearborn
www.worldvision.org
Tim Dearborn serves as Dean of the Chapel and Associate Professor of Theology at Seattle Pacific University, where he is responsible for all campus ministry and urban and global volunteer programs. His interests include church life, leadership, and mission. He has published four books on spirituality and mission, most recently From Mission Tourists to Global Citizens: A Preparation Workbook for Short-Term Mission Teams.